FULL EMPLOYMENT

JOHN H.G. PIERSON, Ph.D.

Prometheus Books

59 John Glenn Drive
Amherst, New York 14228-2197

Published 1996 by Prometheus Books

Full Employment: Why We Need It, How to Guarantee It—One Man's Journey.
Copyright © 1996 by John H. G. Pierson. All rights reserved. No part of this pub-
lication may be reproduced, stored in a retrieval system, or transmitted in any form
or by any means, electronic, mechanical, photocopying, recording, or otherwise,
without prior written permission of the publisher, except in the case of brief quo-
tations embodied in critical articles and reviews. Inquiries should be addressed to
Prometheus Books, 59 John Glenn Drive, Amherst, New York 14228–2197,
716–691– 0133. FAX: 716–691–0137.

00 99 98 97 96   5 4 3 2 1

Library of Congress Cataloging-in-Publication Data

Pierson, John Herman Groesbeck, 1906–
    Full employment: why we need it, how to guarantee it—one man's journey
/ John H.G. Pierson.
        p.   cm.
    Includes index.
    ISBN 1–57392–072–X (alk. paper)
    1. United States—Economic policy—1993–   2. Full employment poli-
cies—United States. I. Title.
HC106.82.P54   1996
339.5′0973—dc20   96–8688
                                                          CIP

Printed in the United States of America on acid-free paper

FULL
EMPLOYMENT

Other Books on Full Employment by John H. G. Pierson

Full Employment (New Haven: Yale University Press, 1941)

Full Employment and Free Enterprise (Washington, D.C.: Public Affairs Press, 1947)

Insuring Full Employment: A United States Policy for Domestic Prosperity and World Development (New York: Viking Press, 1964)

Essays on Full Employment, 1942–1972 (Metuchen, N.J.: Scarecrow Press, 1972)

Full Employment without Inflation: Papers on the Economic Performance Insurance (EPI) Proposal (Montclair, N.J.: Allanheld, Osmun, 1980)

(co-author)

Guaranteed Full Employment: A Proposal for Achieving Continuous Work Opportunity for All, without Inflation, Through "Economic Performance Insurance" (EPI). Selected & Edited from the Writings of John H. G. Pierson by Leonora Stettner (with John H. G. Pierson) (Croton-on-Hudson, N.Y.: North River Press, 1985) *for Harriet-Anne*

Contents

Preface

The power of an idea whose time has come is proverbial. That time may be long in coming, however, when new ideas threaten the dominant position of old ones. This book records the struggle that has already preceded the possible future acceptance of a watershed idea for strengthening our economic system. My own involvement in the story is beside the point, but I couldn't be left out.

J.H.G.P.

Lenox, Massachusetts
April 1996

1

A Sense of Outrage

I was barely awake in my hotel that mid-September morning of 1989. I put the phone down. My wife in America had just told me that the *Washington Post* had rejected my latest article emphasizing the need to guarantee full employment and explaining how to do it. A local newspaper, the *Greenwich Time,* was going to print the piece instead.

Over the next several days the realization of what had happened drove me nearly berserk. All joy went out of the work I was doing— attempting to bring back trees on the Aegean island. In the end I drafted a letter: "Madam: I have a sense of outrage over the *Washington Post*'s rejection of the piece I recently submitted. I want you to know that I am giving the enclosed statement to some of my friends."

My friends were not without influence. The statement I would send them (here shortened a bit) said this:

To Whom It May Concern: The turndown of my article by the *Washington Post* was not just something to be taken in stride. . . . What I have come up against here is cowardice on the part of the *Post*'s editors concerned. . . . I understand, too, how this situation must have developed. . . . When the editors who made the decision refused to give my views a decent hearing—not letting them even be cast in that least implicating form, a letter to the editor—it was because they were afraid that otherwise they would incur the wrath of the dominant wing of the liberal establishment. Certain people there want to continue to think that they already know all the answers. To them newer ideas represent dangerous competition. Their friends in the media can help avert that "danger" by a process akin to denial of free speech. And in this case they did. I would say that the *Washington Post* editors deserve your scorn.

But now there was a technical problem: I didn't know who the editor in question was, so I couldn't properly address my denunciation. To cut delay short, I enclosed my letter and statement in a note to my wife which asked her to fill in the name at the top of the letter and mail it.

That never happened. Frightened by the violence of my language, my wife consulted with a longtime close adviser and with my son, John. Both of them said not to send the letter. She didn't, and instead wrote me her reasoned explanation.

So at least I finally got the name of the *Post*'s editorial page editor via the rejection slip my wife enclosed. But since by that time it was mid-October, I told myself that it was already too late to do anything more. " I feel betrayed by what you have done," I wrote back. "If anyone were keeping score they would now say that the cowardice of [editor] Meg Greenfield—herself no doubt a member in good standing of the group I was talking about, the people who, with or without credentials, already know all the answers—is matched only by the cowardice of myself and my branch of the Pierson family."

Writing then to John, I said I was quite deeply disappointed by *his* part in the action, although "I tell myself that it only happened be-cause the question was sprung on you unexpectedly by phone and you had no time to reflect." This letter ended with "what can I say when even you do not rally in support of my cause?" (John's courage had certainly never been in any doubt and he had always supported my cause—passing articles on to newspaper editor friends for reprinting, suggesting people to contact, and actually helping with editorial suggestions to produce one of my best pieces.)

My wife was anguished. My son wrote back defending the advice he had given as only sensible and rejecting any implication of cow-ardice or disloyalty. In a second letter he called me obsessive. That could well be considered an understatement. My obsession with full employment and my "economic performance insurance" (EPI) method of making it a permanent reality had cost me heavily before this. Friends lost interest. I myself, in my later, post-retirement years, developed a phenomenal lack of attention to most other aspects of life. Now even my family seemed to be coming apart over it.

The questions this raises run in several directions, but at that mo-ment my only question was how it was conceivable for this climac-tic disaster to have happened? So many years of effort had been spent to at least bring my idea for solving the nation's central eco-nomic problem—hub of the wheel, not just one of the spokes—into active discussion. I had sacrificed other prospects and opportunities in straining to achieve this one aim (indeed, I had virtually gambled my whole life on it). My idea had all along received widespread praise from thoughtful and distinguished people. And finally, al-though sick to death of the whole subject and tired as I was at age eighty-three, I had nevertheless flogged myself into writing it up one last time—this weighed heavily on me now.

Some of the praise I had received from well-known persons should be noticed here:

"How nice to read the common sense you always write." (William McChesney Martin)

"I found the views presented in the article of extreme interest." (Lowell Weicker, Jr.)

"I found the idea fascinating, and hope that EPI will get some active discussion." (Abner J. Mikva)

". . . creative and practicable new concepts to achieve the reconciliation of high levels of employment with price stability. They do not call for regimentation or rigid controls." (Robert R. Nathan)

"I have a feeling you are going to make destiny with your concept." (Julius Stulman, head of Lumber Industries, Inc. and publisher of *Main Currents in Modern Thought*)

". . . an important contribution to the current discussion of how to achieve full employment with stable prices . . . the proposal is well worth the consideration of all interested in this most important national problem." (Congressman Richard Bolling)

"I am impressed. . . . I see nothing else that is promising on the horizon." (Robert M. Hutchins)

"A truly inspired book and could not be more timely. . . . To my mind the country is quite ready to require Congress to do something constructive and here you point out both the opportunity and the means." (Wayne C. Taylor)

". . . an eminently practical book taking full note of the political implications and limitations of the U.S. Congress. The book . . . meets very decisively and firmly all arguments that can be brought forward against your proposal." (P. S. Lokanathan)

"Begins where the Employment Act of 1946 leaves off—with a formula for doing what that act said the government should do without saying how." (Rodney Crowther in *Baltimore Sunday Sun*)

"A scheme which can be stated quite briefly in layman's language without becoming patently absurd. . . . As described, it seems both simple and practical." (*V. Kirkus Bulletin*)

"The general trend of your reasoning and counsel seems to me unassailable." (Herbert Feis)

". . . tremendously impressed with it—both from the point of view of good economics and good politics." (Chester Bowles)

"I think it will contribute to the attempt now being made for the first time . . . to establish a coherent theory into which labor's program fits." (Ralph Hetzel, Jr.)

". . . the most intelligent treatment of the subject I have found anywhere, and I hope it will have a profound influence on economists." (George Richmond Walker, businessman)

Gratifying comments, certainly, but almost no help at all in getting my idea actively discussed. What was needed, I had long since been forced to conclude, was the kind of publicity only the media can provide. Especially a major metropolitan newspaper such as the *New York Times* or, better yet, the *Washington Post,* dominant purveyor of news and ideas in our nation's capital.

One would naturally hope that the editors of such newspapers would accept their responsibility to present serious ideas on important subjects to their readers, even when the editors themselves and the particular experts with whom they consorted did not happen personally to agree with those ideas. Why would the editors' own well-worn views be necessarily better then the new ones? Who should be the judge of that—the editors or a wider public? Could the editors in any case legitimately exercise their near-monopoly power to exclude other people's ideas about what our national policies should be? Legitimately or not, that was what was going on. I found myself now the victim of a shocking abuse of power by the *Washington Post,* the latest example of widespread denial of freedom of speech by the Fourth Estate. Without free access to the media, democracy itself broke down. To someone with an idea to promote, the right to be published was what really mattered; the mere right to vote was worthless.

Even the endorsements I received often understated the case, in my opinion. The fact was, the importance I claimed for the idea of which I was the inventor, advocate, and (as I now felt) the trustee transcended all ordinary bounds. No doubt my view on that issue resulted to some extent from sheer visceral defiance of the neglect I suffered from the arbiters of wider public opinion. Its main basis, though, was my own reasoned conviction, repeatedly tested and renewed.

The idea was this: the U.S. Government should adopt a policy of guaranteed full employment, using the device of EPI (economic performance insurance) to make that practicable. This, in my view, offered the best chance of reversing the negative course of history because it would complete an otherwise incomplete and vulnerable American capitalist market system. That is, it would make that system indefinitely sustainable on a decent basis, with justice and opportunity for all at home and a workable degree of harmony with the rest of the world. We could be at a turning point in human affairs. Admittedly, a sensational claim.

There are, clearly, two ways in which a nation's production can be organized: by centralized production planning and by the pull of market demand. Production planning, as in the former Soviet Union, can in principle assure full employment, but it breaks down sooner or later from sheer awkwardness. Furthermore, just as its critics have always said, it becomes intolerable long before it collapses because of its inevitable denial of individual freedom. A market system, as in the American economy, is fundamentally different. It can assure personal freedom and a competitive drive to produce what consumers want—given restraint of monopolies, naturally, and help from a public sector. Yet a market system has a potentially fatal defect, too: no way has so far been found to make sure that everyone has a chance to get into the production act. Indeed, in reality, because of recessions and too much involuntary unemployment even between recessions, many persons do not in modern times (with the frontier long gone) have that chance but are instead excluded from the competitive enterprise game. Life and liberty for all, yes; the pursuit of happiness, only maybe.

What a market system requires above all else is an adequate

market. Not simply a sufficiently large *current* market; plainly, for investment decisions, expectations concerning the market *in future* are even more important. The Achilles heel of the American, and any other, market system is the ever-present fear and frequent reality of a shortage of markets. My proposal was and is for a guarantee of enough jobs to go around, coupled with and (the crux of the matter) made feasible by a confidence-building second guarantee that the market will be held at an adequate level year after year. This would not only assure permanent full employment while at the same time preserving freedom and individual production initiative ("the market is there; get your market share") but it would make progress on all other socially important fronts easier to achieve.

It would also allow our foreign policies to be established on the broadest strategic grounds, freed from the compulsive distortions often brought about in an effort to make up for the failure of domestic policy to deal properly with the markets-and-jobs problem. The magnitude of this further claim, too, can hardly be exaggerated. My claim is that, in a world torn by antagonisms and widely ravaged by poverty and hunger, my proposal would permit us to deal with other nations in a confident, firm, and globally constructive manner. We could be the good neighbor we like to think of ourselves as being, extending aid generously to the developing countries of the Third World and also accepting their exports, so as to let them "move from aid to trade" as soon as possible. In return we would greatly strengthen our chances of coming to satisfactory agreements in the tough North-South debates that loom ahead on such key issues as protection of the environment and control over population and migration.

2

The Protagonist

Anyone who knew me when I was young and rather shy would have noticed two things: I was, generally speaking, intelligent and I was highly motivated. Always top of my class in school, I went on to achieve the highest four-year average in the history of Yale College* up to that time. My motivation for doing a thing like that, and for doing well generally, doubtless came in part from wanting to please my high-minded, somewhat older-than-usual parents. Very likely it also came as a combative reaction to my father's and brother's formidable competitiveness. A feature of my early life in New York City was the evening game of rolling or tossing checker men toward the centers of two rugs in the parlor. I almost invariably lost those contests, which made me furious.

My forebears on both sides of the family had been in America since before the Revolution. Charles Wheeler Pierson, my father, had

---

*The undergraduate part of Yale University.

some doctors and preachers in his ancestral background; was himself raised on a farm in New York state; graduated valedictorian of
his class at Yale; studied law and joined one of the oldest firms in the
city; specialized in Constitutional questions; deplored the growing
tendency for lawyers to become mere errand boys for business; and
occasionally argued cases before the U.S. Supreme Court. He ought
to have been a judge himself, and wanted to be, but lacked the political skill to get the right appointment. My mother, Elizabeth
Granville Groesbeck, dear to all who knew her, was a modest, soft-
spoken person and a talented amateur artist who came east from a
well-connected Cincinnati family. Her great-grandfather, inciden-
tally, had helped in the successful defense of Andrew Johnson at his
impeachment trial. My older brother, George Wilson Pierson, regularly led his classes in studies, too, and went on to become a distinguished historian and for long decades a main pillar of the Yale
community.

Studying was far from being my exclusive interest, however, or
the only leading indicator of where I was headed. I also struggled to
do well in soccer, baseball, and other sports, an aim accomplished
with reasonable success considering that I grew slowly and had a
rather slight build. Francis Tabor, acting headmaster of St. Bernard's
School in New York, where I started out, used to recite some lauda-
tory verses ending with the line "and never knew the word 'defeat,' " which I felt was directed at me. Barclay ("Toot") Farr, head
sports coach at Groton, gave me one of my proudest moments ever
by saying to my parents, "Congratulations on your all-around boy."
At Yale, where I was student president of Phi Beta Kappa and at
graduation was the first-ever winner of both the high scholarship
prize and the one given for "the combination of intellectual achieve-
ment, fine character, and personality," the scope of my ambitions
widened even more. My extracurricular activities ranged far and
wide: some cross-country running and soccer and the freshman rifle
team (I had developed an eagle eye by shooting woodchucks on my

grandmother's farm); the Dramatic Association, *Yale Literary Magazine,* Glee Club, and Whiffenpoofs*; the Elizabethan Club, Pundits, Chi Delta Theta, and Alpha Delta Phi; on the Student Council in my senior year, a Class Deacon, Class Poet. In the end my classmates voted me the "most scholarly" and "most brilliant"; gave me the second largest number of votes for "hardest worker"; third largest for "most admired," "most likely to succeed," "most versatile," and "most modest"; and fourth largest for "has done the most for Yale."

In college I wanted to do well at everything, but without any clear picture of where it was going to lead. The strain of keeping up this effort was relieved by the fact that most people liked me. And I liked them. I enjoyed the one-to-one relationships, but I also felt a remarkably keen sense of identification with my school class and my college class as a whole, and wished we could somehow all stay together afterward. By nature I was capable of extending that fellow feeling to humanity in general, although no glimmer of that was made clear to me until later. Nothing could have been farther from my thoughts while at Yale than the political, social, and economic problems of America or the world. (It was, to be sure, a time when few Ivy League students cared much about public affairs. My roommate, Alfred Bingham, son of a United States Senator, was an exception there. Bingham soon got into the politics game himself, becoming one of the leaders of a third-party movement centered in the Farmer-Labor Political Federation, which briefly challenged the New Deal from the left. But, generally speaking, political consciousness was at a low level for Yale's class of 1927.)

I had a good sense of humor ordinarily, but I never regarded the dashing of my deep hopes or those of anyone else as funny. From somewhere in my genes, moreover, came a dissatisfaction with "easier" successes and an attraction to difficult personal undertakings, provided they seemed in some way grandly important. I cared noth-

---

*A well-known singing group.

ing for the high marks I received in class, I once told my father, except as an indicator that I would also be able to accomplish something that truly mattered. My mother used to say that I could do anything, provided I wanted to. There was sometimes a reckless and (some would say) even Quixotic element in what my attitude led me to attempt. In a spirit bordering on *hubris* I would aim directly at an objective, scorning a roundabout approach and ignoring the limits of my own resources. In the years ahead I would shoot a tiger (in the bad old days when that was thought to be good); climb the Matterhorn with Charles Duell; found an organization called Voices *To* America; launch a shoestring effort at planting trees where they could scarcely be expected to grow; pursue the thoughts of Eastern mystics; . . . *endeavor to solve the unemployment problem.*

One other trait of mine having major importance for this story was my stubborn persistence. Possibly this derived from Dutch ancestors far back on my mother's side.

*   *   *

Time passes. In 1933, I was in poor shape. I had "gone to seed," as a former fellow-editor of the *Yale Lit* put it. Having graduated from college without any clear idea of what should come next (I majored in English), I had spent half a dozen aimless years, first going around the world with a wonderfully exuberant close friend, Winston Childs; then teaching school back at St. Bernard's; and finally, doing historical research for the Consolidated Gas Company of New York.

My plan there had been to do creative writing on the side. Unfocused though I was, there is not much doubt that a writer was what I had hoped to become all along. But that plan had not worked out. Except for a number of poems, some of which went into a slim volume I published a few years later under a pen name, the product just wasn't there. Married, with my first child on the way, and, having turned down an offer that promised quick success in the utilities business, I was without any recognizable clarity in my life or prospects for the future.

I wanted to do some good in the world, something important. As I mulled this over and over, frustrated by the way things stood, I narrowed the choice down to two possibilities. I could go into medicine. My classmate and friend Hannibal Hamlin—lineal descendant of Abraham Lincoln's first vice president—was belatedly doing that after several years spent leading an ornithological expedition in the South Seas. The other option was to get a Ph.D. in economics as a first step to solving the basic problem highlighted by the Great Depression.

Actually I preferred private affairs to public ones. In my own unhappiness I had become more and more disturbed by the amount of personal suffering that I was beginning to see all around me—as though it had not been there all along. "I know . . . that/" ran one of my poems, ". . . /The human race wins out in the end/ . . . But I remember the individual person/ From the oldest times, burned by the wide removal/ Of the actual from the dream." It also happened that economics, at the heart of public affairs, was the one subject that, as an undergraduate student, I had liked the least. On the other hand I now felt pulled in that direction because of the national economic crisis; surely it ought to be possible to find out how to keep depressions from happening. In another place I wrote: "To the faith in theory, that the right theory actually means something/ (For action that means everything),/ To the faith in plans,/ To the faith magnificently firm on the treacherous weak scaffolding/ Of misunderstanding or understanding of details—either one/ . . ."

There came a day in the spring of 1933 when I had to make up my mind whether or not to accept a part-time teaching appointment in the Yale Economics Department. The pay was small, but at least it would be something. The deadline for decision was noon. I sat with Ham Hamlin on the fence in the campus and talked and talked. At ten before twelve I walked to Connecticut Hall and accepted the teaching offer. Then I signed up at the Graduate School. So began for me the grueling business of getting credentials in the field of economics.

The turbulent years of the Great Depression and the New Deal were hard and turbulent ones for me personally, too. Much of my course work for the doctorate was concerned with trivia—necessarily so, no doubt. The textbook I was using to teach Economics 10 to undergraduates appeared to me to be out of touch with current realities. Prominent among those realities were the struggles pitting the rising labor movement, especially the Congress of Industrial Organizations (CIO) under John L. Lewis, against large corporations bent on preventing unionization. I instinctively sided with labor; was active in the Teacher's Union; attended all sorts of meetings—whether in support of Roosevelt's social revolution or against it on grounds of its seeming inadequacy. Here I mingled freely with communists among others, since they were everywhere, actively pushing their United Front. This had repercussions twenty years later in the era of Senator Joseph McCarthy when my appointment to the United Nations Secretariat was temporarily held up while the U.S. government (which had earlier approved my "top secret" clearance) reviewed and dismissed the charge that I had been a communist myself.

Actually the ideas I was developing about needed change were radical in an entirely different way. Two concepts were central to my thinking right from the start. First, that full employment in the sense of job opportunity for all Americans was the pivotal aspect of the many-sided macroeconomic tangle, not just for fundamental human reasons but for our over-all national strategy as well. Not simply because forced unemployment spelled misery for its victims, but also because the effects of its persistence were slow poison for society as a whole. Second, I believed that any solution for business cycles and unemployment would have to be sufficiently consistent with our American way of doing things so that the willingness to accept those new procedures would be established, *built in.*

In addition I felt it necessary to stress from the outset (against voices seeming to claim the contrary) that the solution had to be found in *domestic* policy. Trying to use foreign policy—notably aggressive export promotion and import limitation—as a crutch for domestic policy failure was a mistake. Thus the opening paragraph of my first book (*Full Employment,* Yale University Press, 1941) would read as follows:

> The crux of a sound policy for the United States is the knowledge that domestic measures and domestic measures alone can bring permanent prosperity and full employment. Many are inclined to say that sound domestic policy is one thing and sound foreign policy another. But in the long run the latter is impossible without the former.

Elaboration and defense of those propositions demanded rigorous analysis, obviously, but my *reason* for developing the thesis in the first place was certainly not technical or in any sense academic. I was emotionally involved as well as intellectually. The situation in America was critical. Abroad, the Nazis and Fascists were making things much worse. When Hitler started bombing London in 1939 and English children were being sent to the country to be out of range, I wrote about that, ending with the lines:

> If, when it is over,
> Things stand with the child as may at present be feared,
> . . . May there then be hope in the air, may some of the words
> In the speeches come from those who can understand,
> May the power fall to those who care for the child
> In an absolute way and will move to break forever
> The chains that bind him down.

After fifty years, five books, and some hundred or more explanations in articles and correspondence (not to mention all the office memoranda), my policy proposal for guaranteed full employment via what amounts to taking out an insurance policy on the American economy had undergone some refining but had not in any real way changed from how it looked then.

3

Economic Performance Insurance

I have no quarrel with the best current economic thinking except that it could not, in my opinion, yield the needed permanent solution to the unemployment problem, given the vagaries of politics and the unpredictability of events.

The governmental action called for under the (permanent) solution that I propose would be as follows. First, the general enabling legislation already in place today, i.e., the Employment Act of 1946 as modified by the Full Employment and Balanced Growth (Humphrey-Hawkins) Act of 1978, would have to be further amended. Ever since 1946 the President has been charged with sending to Congress an annual Economic Report which, among other things, sets forth the levels of "employment, production, and purchasing power" needed to carry out the policy of having conditions that would afford "useful employment opportunities, including self-employment, for those able, willing, and seeking to work." However, in Congress the Joint Economic Committee has only been required

27

to study the President's report and issue its own report on it for the guidance of other committees of Congress. Hence the professed aim of this pioneering legislation has had to take its chances. The likelihood of its implementation in Congress, struggling with multiple and often conflicting objectives, has been slim indeed.

Under my proposal, by contrast, actual guarantees would be given. This could be legislated in a simple way by going back to the original 1946 act, making a few small changes (too obvious to require detailing here) in earlier sections, and adding a new section 6 phrased more or less as follows:

Sec. 6. As soon as practicable after the filing of the report of the Joint Economic Committee, the Congress shall by joint resolution of the Senate and the House of Representatives set forth its decisions with respect to:

(a) the minimum and maximum acceptable levels of employment throughout the year in question;

(b) the minimum and maximum acceptable rates of aggregate personal consumption expenditures throughout the year;

(c) the preventive action to be taken by the President if employment should at any time tend to fall below its minimum, or rise above its maximum, acceptable level as defined in (a); and

(d) the preventive action to be taken by the President in case personal consumption expenditures should at any time tend to fall below their minimum, or rise above their maximum, acceptable rate as defined in (b).

With such an enabling law on the books, step two would be taken every subsequent year. The President would recommend levels of national employment and consumer spending—actually, rather narrow bands with lower and upper limits—that in his judgment ought to be guaranteed for the year ahead. (The statistical series now relied on to show what is happening to employment and un-employment—the "Household Survey" of the Bureau of Labor Statistics and the Census Bureau—are certainly not perfect;* they should be improved as that becomes feasible, but this makes no difference here.) Congress would then guarantee the President's proposed numbers, or its own modification of them, and would specify the procedures to be brought into play to keep the actual numbers (when properly adjusted for seasonal variation) in line with those guarantees.

In our world of highly imperfect competition the full employment target would have to be arbitrary, to be sure. Unsustainable upward pressure on wages and prices needs to be avoided, to be sure. However, there is no such thing as a scientifically correct definition of this "full" amount; instead, under EPI, the President and Congress would find, and commit themselves to, a definition that would be viable politically. The underlying concept of course is that there should be no involuntary unemployment above the so-called "necessary frictional" amount, a term that takes into account people just entering the labor market, or laid off temporarily, or moving from one job to another. On the question of what that amount actually is there will certainly be differences of opinion, notably between labor and management. Controversy aside, however, and lobbying duly taken into account, what is clear is that the "necessary frictional" amount of joblessness is larger today than it can be made to be later with the help of improved general education and special retraining programs. Much of it—the *structural* part—occurs in decayed inner cities and other areas with a weak economic base, and afflicts groups with limited skills and mobility, particularly black teenagers. Certainly the government also has a moral obligation to reduce *transitional* difficulties by giving adjustment assistance if jobs are lost as a result of

---

*From time to time special commissions of experts are set up to study the problem and make recommendations. It's anything but an easy task.

action that the government itself has taken—as, for example, when an industry is hard hit by the elimination of longstanding barriers to imports.

Step three—the honoring of the guarantees once they are given —would be a matter of administration, not policy, since the policy would have been decided already. It would therefore be carried out by the President without further intervention by Congress. Designated offices in the executive branch—quite likely the departments of Labor and Treasury—would apply the Congressionally specified procedures *if, as, and when actually needed* for hitting the official targets.

What would those procedures be? The obvious remedy for keeping employment itself from being too low or too high would be a nationwide reserve shelf of public services and public works.* Many of those reserve-shelf jobs would naturally involve federally funded expansions of programs already under way in state, local, and federal budgets, rather than altogether new programs. Types of work capable of being started and tapered off quickly would logically be favored. Congress would have to establish the rules for state-by-state apportionment of any required public works expansions or restrictions.

Keeping *consumer spending* within *its* guaranteed limits, on the other hand, could be handled in a variety of ways. The basic requirement here would be broad and fair distribution of whatever tax or "transfer payment" changes were used for the purpose. For example, Congress might decide that the executive branch must be ready to raise or lower slightly the withholding rate on the personal income tax. (Congress would in that case have first modified our income tax law by adding a negative income tax feature to it—a short step from present earned income tax credits). The credits or al-

---

*When employment levels became too low, existing programs would be expanded and others created to fill the need. When the employment levels become too high, many programs could have their funding reduced or would be suspended temporarily.

lowances would then be raised and the taxes lowered whenever it was necessary to increase consumer spending in order to meet the guarantee, while taxes would be raised and allowances lowered, although presumably never below their base level, in the opposite case. Another practical option would be to institute a standby two-way federal bonus-or-tax procedure at consumer sales points. Here all buyers of goods and services at retail would (for expansion) receive coupons or stamps convertible into cash at a bank or post office or (for contraction) they would have to pay a special federal sales tax. Under either of those illustrative plans, or no doubt under any other plan likely to be adopted, the spending by consumers would be boosted or restrained (i.e., when necessary for making good on the guarantee) by way of actual changes brought about in their "disposable income." Exhorting consumers to help the economy by spending money they do not have would be no part of this scenario.

Again, I am not suggesting that the EPI procedures should *replace* any other useful economic mechanism. For example, the Federal Reserve Board would still need to exercise its judgment on interest rates and money supply. It is simply that the last word on employment levels would be spoken by elected representatives and not by the Federal Reserve.

So much for a bare outline of the governmental action required under my essentially rather simple plan. A parenthetical comment needs to be added here, however. In order to let business as a whole prosper consistently and workers always find jobs, the aggregate of all expenditures for the current output of goods and services, not just consumer expenditures, is the key element to focus upon. This aggregate market, best represented statistically by gross domestic product (GDP), has four component parts: those personal consumption expenditures, which currently amount to roughly two thirds of the total; gross private domestic investment; government purchases (*purchases* only; *other* kinds of government spending do not count here); and net exports of goods and services (a substantial minus quantity today, since our imports greatly exceed our exports). The last three of these components, however, are simply not capable of being guaranteed by government under our economic system, and therefore the solution that I propose is to estimate (a) the needed total market or GDP and (b) the most likely subtotal made up of those other three components, and subtract (b) from (a) to arrive at the amount of consumer spending to be guaranteed. This may sound slightly complex to the uninitiated, but it is not a difficult matter for sophisticated technicians. The President's experts and the ones serving Congress are perfectly capable of using experience as a basis for the guesswork involved and then working out the arithmetic.

To avoid a possible misunderstanding, my plan certainly does not imply that consumer spending should increase, relative to investment. As virtually all economists agree, and as President Clinton emphasizes today, I, too, maintain that the opposite is what is needed. We need more *investment*—both private and public—to make America more productive and more competitive. That change is extremely important and long overdue. Our policies should work to bring it about.

*   *   *

In one of my articles I used the following analogy to help clarify the idea of economic performance insurance (EPI) as a whole for readers who might be allergic to anything even approximating technical economic jargon.

> To understand "economic performance insurance" or EPI, think of our economic system as driven by two engines: production, which provides jobs and generates income, and spending (consumption and investment spending) which motivates production and employment by providing a current and prospective market for goods

and services. Each engine pumps out to the other and each depends for fuel on what the other pumps out. All this is familiar, of course. So is the fact that the system doesn't tend to keep running at a full employment rate automatically, as the classical school assumed.

What is not so familiar is the idea that a balanced circular flow at the full-employment rate, while it won't come about naturally, can nevertheless be created artificially by tuning both engines occasionally so that each reinforces the other with optimum support. Once they are revved up by stages to the right pitch, neither one can easily get very far out of line, and comparatively minor tuning should then suffice. Furthermore, the system's chronic obstructions and leaks will then be considerably easier to identify and correct; hence a prospect of still less tuning. This in essence is the EPI idea.

*   *   *

Another analogy, possibly not too far-fetched, also comes to mind. Adopting the EPI policy would be like introducing the forward pass in football. Except that, with EPI, we would see one completed forward pass after another. In other words, the market is projected ahead and then realized.

4

The Crusade Begins

After five years in the Yale Graduate School I had my Ph.D. It would have taken me less time had I not been teaching in the College, too. My dissertation, "An Essay on the Possibilities of Monetary [actually monetary and fiscal] Control," amounted to little more than finger exercises on the idea I was trying to perfect. Still, I was satisfied to have done it. Better to be in the foothills of the Alps, I felt, than on the very summit of an anthill.

The professor who encouraged me by showing real interest in my evolving idea was James Harvey Rogers. Rogers was then taking frequent trips to Washington to advise President Roosevelt on monetary policy. Unfortunately for our country, and for me personally as well, he died in a plane crash in Rio de Janeiro harbor.

By that time—the summer of 1939—I was just completing a year on a Sterling Fellowship granted by Yale for continuation of my research. Part of that year was spent attending courses at Harvard and writing a report. I was living alone now and headed toward divorce.

Some of my spare time in Cambridge was given to distributing leaflets for the Massachusetts Committee to Defend the WPA (Roosevelt's Works Projects Administration). Critics said that the WPA was just "leaf raking," and Massachusetts Senator Henry Cabot Lodge was among those wanting to kill it off.

Later that year I was in New York, joining with Alfred Winslow Jones in establishing the Institute for Applied Social Analysis, under the sponsorship of the Council for Research in the Social Sciences, Columbia University. The institute's ambitious aim was to answer the following question: What must be done in our country to achieve lasting full employment, at the same time retaining and extending democracy and efficiency? Renowned historian Charles A. Beard agreed to be chairman of the governing board, which also included economist Wesley C. Mitchell, sociologist Robert S. Lynd, and other distinguished social scientists—Eduard C. Lindeman, Mark A. May, Harlow S. Person, Clarence E. Pickett, and George Soule. Jones was Director of Research; I served as Associate Director. Frasier W. McCann provided some money to get the enterprise going.

The plan was to carry out seven selected projects, but the institute while it lasted only got around to two. Under one project heading sociologist Jones conducted a survey of the attitude of rubber workers in Akron, Ohio, toward the conflict between property rights and personal rights and produced a highly successful book titled *Life, Liberty, and Property.* Under project no. 1, "The economic conditions for full employment," I analyzed *Toward Full Employment,* a notable book written by four prominent business leaders—Henry S. Dennison, Lincoln Filene, Ralph E. Flanders, and Morris E. Leeds—and went on to complete my own book, *Full Employment.*

My immediate mentor and critic here was Wesley Mitchell, professor at Columbia University and director of research at the National Bureau of Economic Research. He was a past president of the American Economic Association and was often cited as the father of modern business cycle theory. I didn't quite manage to get Mitchell's flat endorsement for my views on national policy. Mitchell side-stepped, saying that his own work lay in a more technical field—he "had set his hand to the plow and wanted to continue on down to the end of the furrow." However, when the Pabst Brewing Company not long afterward held a national essay contest on how post-war employment problems should be solved, Mitchell was on the board of judges that awarded me one of the seventeen prizes. There were 35,767 entries in that contest altogether.

My *Full Employment* was a reasonably successful book, too, and had a second printing half a dozen years later. Written in the scholarly tradition, it analyzed the various available estimates of the extent of unemployment in the United States from 1920 to 1940; considered the two distinct economic problems of "full" employment and the "optimum allocation" of it; contrasted the alternative approaches of planned production—as in the Soviet Union—and production for market; and described in broad terms the conditions under which full employment could—contrary to past experience—be continuously maintained even in a market economy. I did not go so far as to propose specific legislation. As I put it, "This book . . . is not a program for ending unemployment. It is, rather, *an attempt to set down the conditions under which unemployment would not exist,* and thus to lay necessary groundwork for a full employment program." The book ended on the following cautionary note:

No matter what fiscal methods, or other methods, government proposes to use in behalf of full employment, it would be idle to suppose that misunderstanding, reasonable difference of judgment, self-interest, and sheer prejudice will not raise up a formidable opposition. Indeed it is likely that a political party setting out to abolish unemployment and yet retain democracy will eventually see its efforts defeated unless it possesses to begin with an understanding of public opinion enabling it to find the formula that will really command the broadest popular support, and then moves with resolution in the light of that understanding, shunning the half-measures that, powerless to put an end to depression and idleness, will seem to the nation too high a price to pay for any lesser benefit.

Praise came from several of my professors and fellow students in the Yale Graduate School, and from noneconomists as well. Whitney Griswold, in later years President of Yale but at that time an associate professor of government and international relations, wrote: "I consider this one of the most important books of the year and am willing to bet that it will stand out even more prominently in the perspective of the decade." Oscar Lange, who was then associate professor of economics at the University of Chicago and somewhat of a guru for younger economic theorists in general, said that "Mr. Pierson's book on 'Full Employment' treats the most important economic problem of our times. . . . All the problems . . . are illuminated by his investigation. The manuscript shows that the author is one of the most competent people to write on this subject." Wilmoore Kendall, writing in the *New Republic,* called it "the first book by an American representative of the 'Keynesian' school of economics who is ready to face up to the problem of engineering popular consent for a government policy calculated to eliminate involuntary unemployment from our economic system. . . . Pierson writes, in short, as a majority-rule democrat." Elizabeth F. Baker in the *Survey Mid-Monthly* said that the book "should be pondered by all real democrats who are out to salvage democracy."

But public attention was shifting to the war in Europe. With money for its intended program expansion nowhere in sight, the Institute for Applied Social Analysis closed down. Alfred Jones became an editor of *Fortune* magazine and then went into the investment business, pioneering the hedge fund idea so successfully that he earned a reputation as "the Jones nobody keeps up with." I cast about for a way to step up the campaign I had undertaken to solve America's basic operating problem and put an end to what Wendell Willkie had found a telling phrase for—the new form of slavery that shuts men *out.*

Here I faced another watershed decision, almost without noticing it. Others might well have considered the alternative of going back into academia to be the logical choice. (Rogers of Yale and now Alvin Hansen of Harvard, and later on many others, went back and forth between teaching in a university and advising at the highest levels in Washington.) But that was too slow and too remote a course of action to suit me. I felt the need to come to grips with the employment issue in a practical way there and then. Why wait long years to acquire a professional reputation and a full professorship first? In any case I had never been attracted by the idea of a teaching career. What I wanted was to be an active participant in change.

My former headmaster at Groton, Endicott Peabody, wrote me at this time that "I can conscientiously supply a statement which would, if taken at face value, secure you any position short of that of the President of the United States." Charles Beard wrote: "There are not many people in the world whom I can commend wholeheartedly. You are one of the few whom it is a real pleasure to commend and I hope you will always call on me without any twinges of conscience."

Beard had the idea of giving me a letter of introduction to John L. Lewis. "I like the two-fisted man, in this world of guff and bull," said Beard. So on one of my trips to explore job possibilities in Washington I found myself telling the CIO's redoubtable leader that it seemed not at all clear that the government was really interested in full employment, and asking him whether perhaps the labor movement was more interested. "No," growled Lewis, "the government is *not* interested in full employment; all that the government is interested in is the *war.*" Nothing very helpful came of this interview except that it led to my getting to know the CIO's chief economist, Ralph Hetzel.

On my visits to Washington, just before Americans found themselves in the war, too, I was offered several government jobs. Recruiters were busy building up the staff of half a dozen agencies. ("How old did you say you were? Thirty-five? Wonderful! That's just the ideal age.") But none of those jobs led in the right direction as far as I was concerned. Then one day I met William R. Leonard, a statistician with the Bureau of the Budget. Leonard told me that the number two post was vacant in the Post-war Labor Problems Division, which had recently been established in the Labor Department's Bureau of Labor Statistics (BLS), under a special Congressional grant of funds. The division was created "to conduct studies relative to problems likely to arise upon the termination of the existing emergent conditions in connection with defense activities throughout the United States, in cooperation with the National Resources Planning Board." I applied for and obtained that position and came to Washington the day after Pearl Harbor to start work. About a year later the division's chief, Dal Hitchcock, went into the Army and I became chief.

A year after that, when I was classified 1-A for the draft, my immediate supervisor, the head of the Employment and Occupational Outlook Branch, wanted me held back from military service as a "necessary man." I did not feel that I was necessary in the sense Donald Davenport meant, and my impulse to decline the requested exemption was strong. What I felt more strongly still, however, was that the battle for a full-employment policy was the one in which my contribution to America's future could really amount to something, and so I agreed to stay.

The Post-war Division had up to sixty people in it and a fine *esprit de corps*. A number of the young professionals (economists and statisticians) had their Ph.D.s. The research program included studies of the impact of the war on specific local areas; industry studies, including an "input-output" study of the pre-war American economy, which was mostly conducted at Harvard by a small staff under the direction of Professor Wassily W Leontlef; historical studies of demobilization problems after World War I; and general economic analysis of how full employment could be maintained after the war. This last area was, naturally, where I did most of my own professional work, as distinct from performing my duties as division chief. Under my direction, for example, Marvin Hoffenberg produced "Estimates of National Output, Distributed Income, Consumer Spending, Saving, and Capital Formation" (published in 1943) and Emile Benoit-Smullyan compiled a 250-page "confidential" report that drew on the division's rather elaborate classification of current proposals to analyze the main types of post-war full-employment programs being suggested.

Many widely differing kinds of programs were under discussion in those years. Though the New Deal was over and done with, it was still fashionable and not politically incorrect to think that the unemployment problem, too, should and could be solved. One idea that continued to command attention some time after its first appearance was the plan for concerted industrial expansion under governmental auspices developed by Mordecai Ezekiel, economic adviser to the Secretary of Agriculture. Under his proposal the government would guarantee the markets for specific products (i.e., not the *over-all* market, as in my proposal) and would buy up at prearranged prices, for temporary storage, any products within established quotas that remained unsold.

Then as always, however, it was common practice to claim that a proposed policy that was really aimed in some other direction in the first instance would be a great creator of more jobs, too. More jobs, after all, was what the public especially wanted, so why not emphasize that? On the other hand, attainment of those additional jobs was to be the by-product or side effect of something else. Many such proposals did, as they do today, have job-generating potential, other things being equal. On the other hand, as long as full employment would be targeted only indirectly, with no guarantees given, I noted that those beneficial employment results could always be counter-acted by unforeseen events or by other policies that happened to be in effect at the same time.

The forward-looking businessman's Committee for Economic Development participated actively in the free-for-all economic policy debates. The CED was headed by Paul G. Hoffman of the Studebaker automobile company, soon to be drafted to run the Economic Cooperation Administration under the Marshall Plan, which helped rebuild our allies after World War II. At one of the American Economic Association's annual meetings I was on the program to discuss Hoffman's "Business Plans for Post-war Expansion." Another prominent trustee of CED was Beardsley Ruml, chairman of Macy's, who popularized the slogan "reduce taxes to balance the budget at full employment." I tried without much success to make sense of that phrase. It certainly had rhetorical appeal for anyone interested in lower taxes or a balanced budget or both. It also made a point, important conceptually, about what could be expected *if*—repeat *if*—full employment were in fact achieved: the tax base would be larger than otherwise, so that whatever tax revenues were needed for budget balance would then be obtainable with lower tax rates. But, although Ruml seemed to imply that lowering taxes would somehow in and of itself bring full employment about, there was actually nothing to suggest that that would be the likely result—or that the budget would be balanced either.

5

The Department of Labor

I had no trouble fitting my own writing in with my job at the BLS. Eager to move from theoretical formulation of my idea into practical promotion of it, I produced a variety of short and long articles, and more than a dozen of them appeared in print within the next several years. The first of these was a short piece titled "The National Income Insurance Idea." (The term "Economic Performance Insurance" did not occur to me until many years later.) Alfred Bingham, my close friend and always one of my staunchest supporters, frustrated me this time by not printing it in his magazine, *Common Sense*. However, Congressman Jerry Voorhis of California included it in the "extension of remarks" section of the *Congressional Record* early in 1942. Voorhis, a particularly fine and highly regarded member of the House, will be remembered as the victim of one of Richard Nixon's most vicious political attacks a few years later.

Even before moving to Washington I had dashed off an informal near-book-length-manuscript, "Conversation with Joe," which I hoped would popularize my plan and get it more quickly from theory into action. (" 'Hold on, will you,' said Joe, 'I don't know what you're talking about. Go slow. One thing at a time. Now kindly tell me, to begin with, what you mean by national income insurance. I never heard of it.' ") The National Resources Planning Board now talked about publishing this, but the plan fell through for budgetary reasons.

A more conventional effort was my big article on "The Underwriting of Aggregate Consumer Spending as a Pillar of Full-Employment Policy," which took up thirty-five pages in the March 1944 issue of *The American Economic Review*. Other articles of mine, all on this same subject, appeared in various publications— *The Antioch Review, Life and Labor Bulletin, Free World, World Economics, Monthly Labor Review*, and several others. Some were reprints from speeches; I had speaking engagements at New York University, the University of Michigan, annual meetings of the American Economic Association, and elsewhere.

I was greatly heartened by some of the responses I was getting. "I think it is one of the wisest surveys of the situation and it offers genuinely statesmanlike policies" (Marc A. Rose, associate editor of *The Reader's Digest*). "Nowhere has this point [that the domestic employment problem concerns our foreign policy as well] been better made than in a recent study of post-war employment by John H. G. Pierson" (Charles G. Ross, White House Assistant). "It seemed to me to be the first original contribution in this field of economic thought" (Wayne F. Caskey, economist). "It is exciting reading. . . . Whoever has a less offensive plan of last resort to check the downward spiral ought to let it be known. One should read the Pierson document if only to be scandalized" (Thad Snow in *A Farmer Looks at Fiscal Policy*). "Its realistic and responsible approach . . . is obvious" (Will Lissner in *The New York Times*). "The best thing ever written on full employment, or at any rate the best thing I have seen" (Bushrod W. Allin, Special Assistant to the Chief of the Bureau of

Agricultural Economics). "I believe that your plan comes nearer to a practical program for the preservation of our economic and political system than any other which has come to my attention" (H. Gordon Sweet, businessman). "I am happy to say that I have never been associated with a keener and more constructive thinker" (Professor Emory Q. Hawk, economic historian, the most senior staff member in the Post-war Division itself).

Top-ranking theorists of political economy were more cautious in their assessment. They treated my writings with respect but, to my amazement, some of them simply couldn't seem to understand what it was that I was saying. I was expressing myself in plain English, but somehow it was as though their minds could not get out of the grooves that had been etched by their professional training and experience. They would argue learnedly against positions they thought I had taken but that I hadn't taken at all. For them, presumably, there could be nothing new under the sun. A few years later I tried to dispel some of those baffling misconceptions by contributing an article to the 1949 issue of *The Review of Economics and Statistics** in which I rebutted remarks that had been made at one time or another by Professors Benjamin Higgins, Alvin H. Hansen, and Alan R. Sweezy. I wasn't trying "to argue my position but to clarify it by removing misapprehensions about it, so that future arguments about it may be more fruitful."

For example, this massive misapprehension from Hansen: "Underwriting consumption will not provide full employment. The belief that it will is based on an inadequate conception of the factors on which full employment, in all modern societies, is based. . . . His [my] proposal to underwrite consumption is . . . inadequate (as I believe he himself would admit)." I commented as follows: "Of course, I have never suggested that full employment could be assured by maintaining, let alone merely underwriting, only consumption. In the

---

*"The Underwriting Approach to Full Employment: A Further Explanation."

pamphlet that Hansen cites by title I strongly emphasized that it would also be essential to underwrite total employment as such, and that the effectuation of this further guarantee would bring into play a second balance wheel—namely, expansion and contraction of public works and services."

One of the jobs of the Post-war Division was to work with the American Federation of Labor and the Congress of Industrial Organizations (still separate at that time) on their post-war planning. In 1943, at the AFL's request, I wrote "Employment After the War," which was printed in the *American Federationist* and also became a best-selling pamphlet. In it appeared the following prediction which proved to be dead wrong: "Discharges from the armed forces and from war production will rapidly outrun new job opportunities in peace production. Millions will be looking for work without being able to find it immediately in private industry and normal peace-time operations. This can be stated flatly now." I was almost more pleased than embarrassed when this error showed up two years later. What it did was prove my contention that national policy simply cannot afford to rely on forecasting and needs an "insurance" approach instead. (The only reason this categorical statement was made in the first place was that the jovial and highly competent branch chief to whom I reported was both temperamentally and professionally committed to predicting job prospects. "Our guess is best," read the motto on the wall of Davenport's office.)

I was then designated to prepare a major report for the Labor Committee on National Policy of the National Planning Association, a nonprofit, nonpartisan organization devoted to planning by Americans in agriculture, business, labor, and government. The committee was made up of AFL, CIO, and Railroad Brotherhood members. Clinton S. Golden of the United Steelworkers was chairman. When this report, *Fiscal Policy for Full Employment,* came out in 1945, J. Raymond Walsh, WMCA radio commentator who had been CIO's economic research director after Hetzel, told his audience:"Yesterday there was released what is far and away the most significant and competent document in the history of the organized labor movement." My EPI proposal was a major feature of this report.

My campaign also spilled over into time away from my job. Shortly before the end of the war I spent several weekends with my closest associate, Benoit-Smullyan, inventing a "Jobs for All" board game somewhat resembling Parcheesi®. Players would become postwar planners in Washington, running into various problems and pitfalls and adopting various policies that would either help or hinder them in getting through demobilization and reconversion to Full Employment. A hefty accompanying book of rules and explanations detailed the foreseeable effects of the many different policies. (The game of course got my special twist: a player lucky enough to land on space 55, marked "Try for Guarantee of Job Opportunity and Consumer Market" went to the "inside track" which gave him or her the chance to get to Full Employment very quickly.) Several leading manufacturers of games decided not to gamble on this one. I then tried to get *Life* and *Look* magazines to carry the story and a picture of the board in a double-page spread, but that effort didn't succeed either, although some of *Life*'s editors showed considerable interest.

The Post-war Division was liquidated late in 1944 on my recommendation. Much of its statistical work had by then become closely integrated with the regular programs of the permanent units of the Bureau of Labor Statistics. Besides that, Acting Commissioner Ford Hinrichs wanted to center the economic *policy* work in his own office. I was named his consultant.

My outside contacts and participation in conferences expanded. By virtue of working for the Department of Labor, I was chairman of the interdepartmental committee on Full Employment and Economic Foreign Policy, which had representation from the State Department, Treasury, Commerce, Agriculture, Labor, Tariff Commission, Office of Price Administration, etc. I served on the Foreign Investment Policy Committee reporting to the President's Executive

Committee on Economic Foreign Policy. I was the chief draftsman of a confidential report on full employment policy prepared by a joint committee for the secretaries of Commerce and Labor. I was in a small official American group that held meetings—secret at the time—with Lord John Maynard Keynes and other prominent British economists to discuss common interests in resolving post-war employment problems.

Out of the welter of discussion of the jobs question during those wartime years there finally emerged the Employment Act of 1946. As it eventually shaped up it was weak enough to suit its opponents; yet it was and remains a landmark in the symbolic sense and a foundation on which a solid structure could easily be built at some future time, given the will to do it.

For all his unforgettable accomplishments Franklin Roosevelt never got rid of unemployment; only the war did that. Now the idea was in the air that large-scale unemployment should simply not be allowed to return. A bill was introduced in the Senate by four Democrats (Murray, Wagner, Thomas of Utah, and O'Mahoney) and was cosponsored later by four Republicans (Morse, Tobey, Aiken, and Langer). In the House, Democrat Wright Patman from Texas introduced a similar bill and was joined by more than a hundred others. Hard struggles followed, especially in the House. The watered-down bill as agreed to in conference committee was passed by an overwhelming bipartisan vote. President Truman signed it.

Behind the scenes a number of widely differing drafts had been drawn up by a succession of presumed experts and approved or taken apart at discussion sessions mostly held in the offices of Senator Murray or Senator Wagner. A climactic moment arrived when something had to be done about a strong draft declaration clearly at odds with a weak draft operating section. That is to say, a powerfully worded preamble, consistent with Senator Murray's original presentation of "a bill to establish a national policy and program for assuring continuing full employment" still said that the job of maintaining full employment really had to be done; but this on the other hand came up against second thoughts to the effect that nothing must fundamentally change. At that point something clearly had to give way. As might have been expected (so early in our American consideration of the pivotal importance of the opportunity to work), the dilemma was resolved not by toning the operative section up but by toning the preamble down.

I was not invited to write any of those preliminary drafts. Instead, I wrote memos with the help of which Hinrichs attempted to persuade the new Secretary of Labor, Lewis B. Schwellenbach, Frances Perkins's successor, to do two things: throw the department's weight onto the scales to improve the text of the bill, and set up a Cabinet Committee on Full Employment in the government's executive branch. Schwellenbach remained unconvinced, however, that it was up to him to intervene in a vigorous way in either the drafting or the subsequent implementation of this law.

How anything could be of greater concern to the Labor Department than its implicit obligation to protect the opportunity to work, or labor, was hard for me to imagine. However, Schwellenbach's caution was perhaps understandable in the light of the immediate economic outlook. Wartime "pent up" demand had been let loose. Far from soaring to anything like pre-war heights, unemployment stayed below four percent for three years after V-J Day before turning upward again. At the same time prices were climbing quite rapidly, and Truman was focusing on the need to combat inflation rather than unemployment. I here made the unoriginal discovery that long-range thinking is out of fashion in Washington. The general rule there is that you can't fix the roof when it's raining, and when it isn't raining you don't need to. Also, in any recession, when an up-turn is perceived, you must relax and stop looking for a solution to the recession problem.

My own proposal, it should be pointed out, was expressly calculated to curb inflation as well as unemployment. My book, for example, had argued at some length that the ceilings to be imposed on total consumer spending and on employment itself (along with the all-important floors to be put under them) would certainly give strong support to efforts to hold prices down. But evidently—and this was only the first of many such reminders—that part of my message had not been stressed sufficiently in my writings. It didn't sink in.

In 1946, I moved out of the BLS to become economic adviser to Assistant Secretary of Labor David A. Morse. In that position, and then as special assistant when Morse was promoted to Under Secretary, I found my work lying largely in the field of international negotiations. This suited me well enough because of the way the domestic and international mechanisms are connected. Specifically—other aspects aside—I saw that assured full employment in the United States, dominant player in international economics, was a precondition for obtaining satisfactory accommodations with trading partners.

The game was being played out in the years just before and during the International Trade Organization conferences of 1946–48. Cordell Hull, Roosevelt's secretary of state, had been negotiating tariff reductions, etc., during the 1930s on a *bilateral* basis, country by country. Harry C. Hawkins and his Trade Agreements Division did the spadework for it. Now Hawkins chaired a committee charged with preparing a draft that would serve as the basis for negotiating a comprehensive *multilateral* agreement worldwide. This committee in turn had a number of subcommittees, of which my committee on Full Employment and Economic Foreign Policy was one. Thus, when the time came, I served as a delegate representing the United States on the multinational committee on Employment and Economic Activity which prepared one of the chapters of what became the Havana Charter of a to-be-established International Trade Organization. Maintenance of fair labor standards was dealt with here as well. I also served for a time on the Economic Development Committee, the main focus of interest for the less developed countries, as that committee began to write from scratch a chapter which the U.S. draft had omitted.

But first I found that it took no small effort to convince our *American* delegation that the attainment of its main objective, trade barrier reduction, would not be enough to take care of the employment problem, too. Some State Department members and others seemed wedded to the idea that it would. Tariff Commissioner Lynn Edminster, for instance, argued strongly that tariff reduction would bring full employment. I and other members of my interdepartmental subcommittee—Arthur Smithies and Walter Salant especially—explained why it would not, or, in other words, why action for full employment had to be taken *independently.* Edminster was slightly baffled: "But you need tariff reduction for *productive* full employment." This at least put him on firmer ground, although other factors such as education, health, and of course technology obviously play important parts too in making the work of employed workers more productive.

As the first International Trade Organization preparatory meeting opened, the London newspapers made it abundantly clear (as I had expected) that Great Britain was not so much enamored of lower tariffs and other trade barrier reductions as it was desirous of having full employment in the United States, so that Americans would be able to buy British products. Some sample headlines: "Britain's 'No' to America on Trade Plans: We Want Guarantees First Against Wall Street Slump"; "Importance of Full Employment"; and "World Trade Hinges on U.S., Briton Asserts: Full Employment Necessary." Delegates from a number of other countries echoed those sentiments as the discussions got under way. Later the representatives from India, Brazil, and other less developed countries said that full employment in itself was insufficient for their countries: what they needed was *productive* employment and hence economic development, modern technology, industrialization. So it was agreed to revise the agenda and set up the above-mentioned separate committee to deal with that subject.

At the second preparatory meeting, in Geneva in 1947, I encountered a different sort of problem: verbal landmines had to be avoided. After strenuous arguments, which as it happened had been almost entirely conducted in English, the English text of the employment chapter was finally adopted. The key clause in it read as follows: "Each member shall take action designed to achieve and maintain full and productive employment and large and steadily growing demand within its own territory through measures appropriate to its political, economic, and social institutions." Next morning a French translation, which (in accordance with United Nations rules) would be equally authoritative, was about to be adopted without discussion when I pointed out that it contained a commitment that was not the same at all, since it said that "Each Member shall achieve and maintain full and productive employment. . . ." Over the French delegate's protest that, in French, that wording meant exactly the same as the English wording did in English, the necessary alteration was made in the French text. (I quite obviously wanted the U.S. Government to commit itself to achieve and maintain full employment, but to commit itself internationally before deciding to do it domestically was unthinkable.)

I was gaining momentum. Clair Wilcox, chairman of the U.S. delegation, praised my "grasp of [the] material, originality in devising solutions, and stubbornness and diplomacy as a negotiator." Harry Hawkins "found in [Pierson] a genuine zeal for the public interest such as I have rarely encountered in any other individual." Ewan Clague, the new Commissioner of Labor Statistics, wrote: "I think that the Department and the Nation will have a hard time finding as able a representative at international conferences as [you have] been."

I went on to play a prominent part at the final Havana Conference, and ventured to imagine that I would be offered a top post in the full-employment part of the International Trade Organization when it was established within the United Nations family of organizations. If so,

I would acquire some real leverage and would perhaps be able to make things happen in Washington. I spoke with Chairman Edwin Nourse of the President's Council of Economic Advisers, which was now functioning under the Employment Act, about the newly demonstrated foreign-relations importance of U.S. full employment. Nourse appeared to be impressed. On other international fronts I was active, too. I was one of two U.S. government delegates joining labor and industry delegates at the first meeting of the International Labor Organization's Petroleum Industry Committee; I was an adviser to Isador Lubin, representing the United States on the new United Nations Economic and Employment Commission; I was a member of the United States delegation at one of the early sessions of the UN Economic and Social Council at Lake Success, Long Island.*

Also, in 1947, the Public Affairs Press published in Washington a collection of my recent writings and speeches, under the title *Full Employment and Free Enterprise.* All things considered, in spite of setbacks, my campaign seemed to be moving into high gear.

---

*Pending completion of the United Nations Building in New York City, the international organization established itself at Lake Success.

6

Foreign Aid

I was in for some disappointments. The U. S. Congress killed the International Trade Organization by failing to ratify the Havana Charter, and instead accepted only a more restricted General Agreement on Tariffs and Trade, better known as GATT. The Public Affairs Press went into bankruptcy before many copies of *Full Employment and Free Enterprise* were sold.

Actually, those disappointments came on the heels of several others. Since the Secretary of Labor wouldn't take a strong position on full employment, I had been trying to gain some other point of vantage in Washington and had had no luck with it. My first choice was the three-member Council of Economic Advisers, newly created by the Employment Act of 1946, but I lacked a powerful sponsor to secure for me one of those presidential appointments. Leon Keyserling, who did manage an appointment to the Council (which he later headed), urged me to Join the Council's staff, but I was too proud to accept subordinate status in the field of my special competence. The

55

other position in which I thought I might be able to influence policy was the staff directorship of the Congressional Joint Committee on the Economic Report, also newly created by the Employment Act. I talked to Senator Robert A. Taft about my interest in obtaining that post, but it, too, went to somebody else.

A third possibility presented itself when Dave Morse was promoted to Undersecretary of Labor. Hoping to succeed Morse as Assistant Secretary, I flew to Miami, where the American Federation of Labor was holding its annual convention, and asked for the endorsement of AFL President George Meany. Meany with great cordiality said that he would have liked to be able to help but that he had already promised to support the candidacy of Philip M. Kaiser, who was Morse's Executive Assistant. The job went to Kaiser.

Perhaps, I thought, it was time to turn away from government service. I applied for a Guggenheim Fellowship, indicating that I would use it to write a popular book on full employment. In March of 1948, I visited the Secretary of the John Simon Guggenheim Foundation, Henry Moe, who told me that they were granting me a fellowship and would let it go through in spite of my uncertainty about using it immediately. A week later, however, when the formal notices were issued, mine said "not granted."

Undersecretary Morse served briefly that year as Acting Secretary of Labor, then was named Director-General of the International Labor Organization (ILO) in Geneva. I left the Labor Department, too, wrote articles, and got married again. For a while, as I juggled various prospects, my wife was the only breadwinner, working as an executive officer in the Food and Agriculture Organization of the United Nations (FAO) until it voted to move its headquarters from Washington to Rome.

If it had come to the point where no good place whatever for advancing my cause was in sight, I was open to proposals for creating such a place myself. A suggestion to that effect came from Mrs. Anne Page, long active in government economic work and in labor and several prominent membership organizations. Her idea was that I should be dean of a graduate school of labor, to be established preferably at Columbia University under its incoming president, General Dwight D. Eisenhower. Her concept was supported by Marion Hedges, an expert on labor-management relations, author, and director of research of the International Brotherhood of Electrical Workers of the AFL. I took soundings with Lloyd Garrison, Ray Walsh, Arnold Zurcher, Oscar Cox, Wayne Taylor, General John H. Hilldring, Robert Calkins, and several others and found that the idea had strong support. Labor education was a live issue. A bill to establish a Labor Extension Service in the Department of Labor was under discussion in Congress. Labor education programs had been set up at a number of colleges and universities, and some of them (Yale, Harvard, Chicago, Cornell, Rutgers, the Michigan Extension Service) were making noteworthy contributions. Yet a new and more ambitious approach seemed to be called for.

"There is a great need," my Washington associates and I wrote, "for an Advanced School of Labor qualified to serve as a national center for research, teaching, and consultation on labor matters. Connected with some major university in a metropolitan area, such a school would train labor administrators and experts for government, trade union, and business service; train teachers in labor education; promote understanding of labor-management relations; serve as a consultant to government on current labor issues, international as well as domestic; engage in research on man's relation to work in the broadest sense."

What appealed to me more than all the rest of it put together was the opportunity it would provide to build a sophisticated understanding in labor circles of the full-employment issue. The curriculum would certainly have a section devoted to that subject. According to our prospectus, "The curriculum should recognize that a general sense of insecurity about the ability of the American economy to continue providing enough job opportunities and avoid recurrence of depression is the most fundamental problem today. This means early emphasis on the study of how to solve this problem; also on exploring the wide implications once the scourge and fear of depression are lifted."

John Gilbert Winant, former governor of New Hampshire, F.D.R.'s first chairman of the Social Security Board, and then his wartime ambassador to Great Britain—a man who reminded people of Abraham Lincoln—was the person whose support most encouraged me to go ahead with this project. I had come to know Winant in London, briefing him day by day on progress in the employment and economic development committees on the proposed ITO charter. Now it came down to how to present the project to Eisenhower himself. Finding the general hard to catch up with, Winant advised me that the best chance of reaching him would be through his brother Milton, in Kansas City. However, as I learned from the State Department, Milton Eisenhower had gone to a United Nations Education, Scientific, and Cultural Organization (UNESCO) conference in Mexico City. I asked Winant by phone: Would it be better to follow him there or wait for his return? In one of Winant's last tactical judgments before his death by his own hand, he urged me to seize the moment and go down. I flew to Mexico City that night, spoke with Milton Eisenhower the next day, and found myself presenting the labor school project to General Eisenhower in the Pentagon two weeks later. This was in November 1947, just before I went to Havana as the Labor Department's designee for the final ITO conference.

General Eisenhower told me that he was very much interested personally but unable to make any decisions regarding the university until he took office there. What was needed was a study to prepare a detailed, polished plan that could be considered by any major university. (A prospectus for such a study, with a budget, had already been prepared by me and my associates.) But first I should talk with Tom Watson.

At that interview in the IBM office when I returned from Havana, the head of the company, Thomas J. Watson, Sr., talked virtually nonstop about his business philosophy and other subjects of interest to him (e.g., why not forget the labor school idea and develop a school for top business executives instead?). In this way he effectively prevented me from elaborating on the subject supposedly at hand. Watson sent word later that he was very much interested in the proposal, but he repeated that any action on it would have to await Eisenhower's installation as Columbia's president in June. Frustrated, I wrote to Eisenhower withdrawing the project from consideration "for the present." Nevertheless, Page, Hedges, and I kept it alive for a few months longer, concentrating on a search for money for the preliminary study. I even wrote to Eisenhower about it again and learned from his aide, Major Cannon, that "I know personally of his continuing interest in your project and his hope that ultimately something can be accomplished." But that was about the end of it. In the meantime the establishment of the Graduate School of *Business* of Columbia University had been announced with considerable fanfare.

Nearly a year later I finally had a new job, thanks to an offer from Wayne Taylor, who had held a number of high government posts—Assistant Secretary of the Treasury, Undersecretary of Commerce, and President of the Export Import Bank among them—and was now Assistant to the Administrator of the Economic Cooperation Administration (ECA), Paul Hoffman. Our European allies were struggling hard, with Marshall Plan aid, to rebuild their war-shattered economies and bring their external accounts back toward balance. A special mission, led by Taylor and composed of officials of ECA and the Commerce Department, went to Europe to see what could be done to speed that balancing process. The *Report of the ECA-Commerce Mission* concluded that the job could be done, that it should be done by expanding European exports rather than by shrinking European imports from the United States, and that a number of specific steps to achieve the purpose could be taken by European governments, European business and labor, U.S. business and labor, and the Organization for European Economic Cooperation.

My part in this was to write the analytical first chapter of the report. An early paragraph read:

> Other countries simply are not earning enough dollars to pay for what they import from us. They have a "dollar shortage." We have a vast export surplus [how ironically this reads today], which we maintain by subsidies at the taxpayer's expense. The problem from everyone's point of view is the problem of the "dollar gap."

Further on came cautionary words about a new problem that would be created by solving the old one:

> With regard to purchasing power, production, and employment in the United States, clearly, as we proceed to narrow or close the dollar gap and so reduce or eliminate our export surplus . . . we give up the stimulus which the excess foreign demand provides. . . . In the process of closing the dollar gap, therefore, it is fundamental that attention must all the more be given, by the appropriate agencies, to domestic prosperity policy, including the maintenance of an overall market—domestic and foreign combined—adequate in size to absorb the output flowing from our tremendous production capacity.

I hit this same point hard in a widely circulated memorandum titled "On Maintaining U.S. Prosperity While Closing the Export-Import Gap":

> (1) Closing the dollar gap will make maintenance of U.S. prosperity and full employment more difficult, regardless of whether the gap is closed chiefly by expansion of imports or by contraction of exports. (2) Expansion of imports will cause comparatively less difficulty than contraction of exports. (3) Domestic fiscal measures

can offset the adverse effects of closing the dollar gap. (4) Domestic fiscal measures should go farther and assure a full-employment volume of demand at all times. A shortage of demand, which may also be created by factors quite unrelated to foreign trade, will arouse such opposition to increased imports and reduced exports as to threaten a gap-closing policy with defeat.

Truman's historic "Point Four" declaration committed our nation to "making the benefits of our scientific advances and industrial progress available for the improvement and growth of underdeveloped areas." A new era opened. In an address in 1950 to the American Academy of Political and Social Science, I analyzed Point Four's relationships with the dollar gap and with full employment. Point Four, I said, "will help postpone the necessity of entirely closing the export-import gap and will facilitate, within limits and for a time, the maintenance of prosperity and full employment in the United States. A sound domestic full-employment program, however, is essential to a proper perspective on Point Four, and to adequate funds for carrying it out, as well as essential to a closing of the dollar gap, especially at the desirable high export-import level. Point Four should be supported for its own sake, and not for specious or extraneous reasons."

Several senators had me on their list of people they consulted about economic legislation. Now Senator Murray introduced the Economic Expansion Act of 1949 in an effort to combat the recession, accompanied by rising unemployment, that the Employment Act of 1946 was intended to prevent but couldn't. His draft bill was long and elaborate, went through several versions, and failed to pass. I offered detailed comments on specific sections of the bill, as Senator Murray requested, and under general criticism I wrote this: "As I see it, the time has come to go beyond the assembling of measures designed to lift employment, production, and purchasing power and proceed to write a law that will give the assurance that full employment will actually be maintained indefinitely. Contrary to rather widely prevailing opinion, I believe that this can be done within the framework of our free system. This bill does not do it. The method which seems to me appropriate is explained below. . . ."

That summer of 1949 the magazine section of *The Christian Science Monitor* featured an article of mine that began as follows: "Current events are stirring up the dormant interest in full employment. More and more people are beginning to say that something had better be done." But nothing significant *was* done.

*   *   *

In 1949, I had to move away from activities in which I could promote guaranteed full employment as part of my paid job. Harlan Cleveland, Deputy Assistant Administrator of ECA, invited me to transfer to a division that was just being formed to extend ECA's interests to Asia. After the communist takeover in China, Secretary of State Acheson had asked Allen Griffin, publisher and editor of *The Monterey Peninsula Herald,* to lead a small mission to Southeast Asia to see whether funds left over from a China program could be used to good effect "in the general area of China not under communist control." The answer (no doubt foreordained) was yes. Griffin came to Washington to head a new Far East Program Division. I became his Chief Economic Adviser and then Policy Adviser.

What this meant was that I helped plan aid programs in six Southeast Asia countries—China/Taiwan, Philippines, Vietnam, Indonesia, Thailand, and Burma—and worked on requests for further Congressional appropriations. The programs consisted of technical assistance backed up by modest amounts of physical equipment, with bulk commodities added in the case of China/Taiwan, where the severe balance-of-payments problem created a situation resembling the one already familiar to ECA in Europe.

I would accompany my chief to Capitol Hill, carrying briefcases stuffed with statistical data which I fervently hoped I could find the right place in should Griffin lean over and say to me, "What's the answer to that one, John?" Allen Griffin was an extraordinarily honest witness. The "Point Four" section in the State Department, which was running another aid program (this one limited to technical assistance), thought nothing of claiming that it was achieving all manner of success, even in cases where its work was still only in the planning stage. In sharp contrast, Griffin, when asked whether he thought that *his* programs were really doing any good, would most likely say, "Actually, Senator, I don't think we've even got to first base so far."

Griffin's honesty slipped a bit in a letter of introduction he gave me to present to Malcolm MacDonald, Commissioner-General for the United Kingdom in Southeast Asia. In 1952 Griffin sent me on an inspection trip to the four remaining country missions. (Burma and Indonesia had dropped out when ECA was converted to the Mutual Security Agency [MSA] with acceptance of U.S. economic aid now made conditional on a willingness to accept U.S. military aid as well.) Griffin's letter contained the exaggerated statement that "There is probably no other person in Washington as familiar with U.S. relationships with Southeast Asian countries as Mr. Pierson."

I completed my mission, although the proposed incidental meeting with MacDonald in Singapore failed to take place, MacDonald having been temporarily called back to London. Griffin returned to his base in California, tired of the way the Washington bureaucracy worked and wanting also to be free to support Eisenhower's candidacy for President of the United States. I soon resigned, too, declining an offer to be Economic Adviser in MSA's mission to China/Taiwan. I had become more or less disaffected with MSA for two reasons. First, I had come to think that most help to the less developed countries ought to be put on a multilateral basis, through the United Nations. The often lower efficiency of those multinational operations would be more than offset by their greater disinterestedness and hence better acceptance by the aid recipients. Second, I was appalled by the way Washington decided what was best for other countries without listening to what *they* thought—or even paying enough attention to the views of its own representatives doing the actual work in the field. Washington always talked, never listened.

7

The United Nations Secretariat

Those views helped shape my career for more than a decade. In 1953, I moved to New York and founded a private organization incorporated the following year as Voices *To* America, Inc. Voices *To* proposed to use mass media of all kinds to promote a better understanding in the United States of the problems and attitudes of other countries. I was president. Associated with me on the board of directors were Ernest Angell, lawyer and chairman of the American Civil Liberties Union; Eric Haight, a college classmate of mine who was president of Films, Inc. and had good media connections; F.S.C. Northrop, Yale philosophy professor and author of *The Meeting of East and West*; Wayne Taylor; and James Gamble Rogers, Jr., an investment banker.

It was an exciting venture. I worked indefatigably on policy, program ideas, and sample scripts. Our group developed a wide range of contacts with writers, film and television experts, area specialists, network executives, foundation officers, and other interested persons including Chester Bowles, Ralph Bunche, John Dickey, Frank Altschul, Robert Redfield, Louise Leonard Wright, Arthur Lall from India, and James Barrington from Burma, to name just a few. Edward R. Murrow used his influence to request funds for a preliminary study from the Ford Foundation. James A. Michener said he was probably coming on the board, but decided he was too busy. Adlai Stevenson, contacted by Angell, showed enough interest to sustain the board's hopes that he would someday be the commentator for the TV news program that was envisaged as the Voices *To* America centerpiece, giving a "third dimension" to the news. Robert M. Hutchins, who was then president of the Fund for the Republic, was interested in considering that same anchorman role, and he and I thought for a time that we saw a way to get the program started with the combined help of Columbia University and *The New York Times*.

It didn't fly. Scraping bottom financially, I had to withdraw and find a paying job. I sent my résumé to a number of business firms with overseas connections. At that moment William R. Leonard luckily appeared from nowhere to solve my personal employment problem for the second time! Bill Leonard had by that time left U.S. government service himself to become chief statistician for the United Nations. He now urged me to apply for the job of Director of the Research and Planning Division in the UN's Economic Commission for Asia and the Far East (ECAFE). I jumped at the chance and was on my way to Bangkok early in 1955. Voices *To* America existed a little longer, and I continued to correspond with it and on its behalf. But finally there was no way of denying that this project, for all its promise, would never get off the ground.

Before leaving America for Bangkok, I found time to write a short technical paper amplifying my explanation of one aspect of my guaranteed full employment proposal. If total employment itself fell below its underwritten level, the answer clearly lay in having government at various levels around the country activate (at federal government expense) various public works and services that were "on the reserve shelf." But how—the question kept recurring—would consumer spending be boosted if *it* fell below *its* underwritten level? I had previously tended to suggest tax reductions or offsets of various kinds, but here I described in some detail the mechanics of an alternative method that would use coupons or stamps, redeemable in cash. These "consumer sales premiums" would be given out in connection with all purchases of consumer goods and services whenever an official "pay out" period had been declared. This paper of mine was published as a Communication in the September 1955 *American Economic Review.*

At ECAFE in Bangkok, P.S. Lokanathan was executive secretary. I had come to know the former editor of *The Indian Economist* quite well at the ITO meetings. Under him and later under another Indian, C.V. Narasimhan, I spent four years directing the commission's economic work. It was an altogether fascinating experience. My staff of about sixty people consisted almost entirely of Asians—economists from virtually all the countries on or near the continent's eastern and southern rim, together with general service helpers mainly from Thailand itself. My division's job was to get out a rather massive annual *Economic Survey of Asia and the Far East*; hold multinational planning meetings; advise generally on various aspects of economic development strategy; and write technical reports. I wrote and edited endlessly. Luckily for me, the working language was English.

The *Survey* was compiled on the basis of short field trips to national capitals by senior staff members, supplemented with last-minute correspondence. (U.S. delegates to ECAFE conferences regularly reprimanded me for including the most populous country in the world, mainland China, citing the fact that field trips there were impossible; what was done instead was to draw on an extensive file of Chinese newspaper clippings kept by my deputy, H. D. Fong.) Filled with statistics—some of dubious validity but nevertheless the best obtainable anywhere—this yearly report was printed at break-neck speed in Hong Kong. The conferences and working parties brought together a wonderful array of young professionals, earnestly striving to find knowledge they could take back with them to raise standards of living at home. What they got out of it might sometimes have been short of perfect illumination, but, as Lokanathan would say, "the better is the enemy of the good." This work and that of ECAFE's other divisions undoubtedly did help the member Asian countries. And, financially speaking, it was done on a shoestring.

I returned to New York in 1959. I was proud of the silver box in-scribed to me by the members of the Research and Planning Division "in appreciation of his inspiring leadership." I was glad, too, that my Burmese friend, U Nyun, who succeeded Narasimhan as executive secretary, wanted me to stay on in Bangkok as his deputy. But, as I explained, my deepest commitment was to the full-employment pol-icy I hoped to see established in my own country, and it was now time to get back within closer range of Washington.

My return to America was handled awkwardly, to say the least. It was not my prerogative, naturally, to select the place of my as-signment. However, when Philippe de Seynes, the Undersecretary for Economic and Social Affairs, was in Bangkok shortly before that time, I told him of my desire to rotate back to New York and got, as I thought, de Seynes's agreement. Later de Seynes forgot that con-versation and demurred. Now able to risk my salary, thanks to an in-heritance, I said that I was coming back anyway. On arriving at UN headquarters I was called before the secretary-general and asked to explain myself. Dag Hammarskjold spoke to me rather sternly but al-lowed my move to stand.

I was first assigned as special consultant to another American, Julia Henderson, who headed the Bureau of Social Affairs under de Seynes. One report of which I was the chief author dealt with the ex-tent to which some forty rich, poor, and intermediate-income coun-tries were balancing their *economic* development drive with efforts and expenditures on *social* needs—health, education, housing. The theory and practice of rural community development were the focus of another study, one that took me to conferences in Asia, Africa, and Latin America. In a third project I joined with representatives of FAO and ILO in preparing a report on land reform.

After completing those tasks, I obtained a year's leave of absence, which I spent—still commuting from Connecticut but working in the UN library—writing my third book about full employment. Until then my opportunities to move that campaign ahead had been more limited than I had hoped they would be once I was back in the States. A small step was taken in 1960 in an article on "An International Economic Code: A Suggestion," which was published in the Swiss magazine *Kyklos.* There I explored the possibility, and possible usefulness, of obtaining under UN auspices a declaration of general principles that would link together the numerous different and sometimes conflicting economic aims of different countries, full employment among them. The ITO experience provided a partial model. The idea would be to establish, in the pursuit of those disparate aims, "priorities" that would be regarded as reasonable in the light of two overriding objectives of the world community as a whole: greater international accommodation and higher and more equal economic development.

In 1960, I also tried to gain the attention of President-elect John F. Kennedy. My letter began as follows: "For many years I made a special study of how the United States could avoid recurring depressions and maintain continuing full employment, and worked actively on this problem in Washington during the war and when the Employment Act was passed. Among economists who advocated measures to try to maintain full employment, I think I can claim that I was the only one who said it was feasible—under our system—to put it in the form of a guarantee. I will not go into the proposed measures here, but wish to call attention to the existence of these proposals and to ask that they be given consideration. To my mind they are still applicable and desirable. . . ." Whoever was screening JFK's mail probably tore up my letter. At any rate no acknowledgment came back.

Barely finished with my year's leave, I was asked to take on a challenging assignment. Early in 1963 the United Nations Conference on Science and Technology had been held in Geneva. Representatives of many developing countries attending that conference felt that assistance with modern science and technology, which could be the most powerful force in the world for raising their standards of living, was not getting the attention it should in the UN set-up; a new agency should be established, they said, and given a mandate in that field. However, since virtually all the agencies in the UN "family of organizations" were already dealing with science and technology in the areas of their special competence, a new agency would clearly have to duplicate, or else eviscerate, the old ones. Someone was needed to assist Secretary General U Thant and Undersecretary de Seynes in handling this issue. Alfred G. Katzin, who had been at the conference, couldn't do it since he was retiring. The task fell to me.

It was decided that an eighteen-member Advisory Committee on the Application of Science and Technology to Development should come into being and should serve as the UN's top advisory committee on the general strategy to be followed in that vital area. Its members would be appointed by the Economic and Social Council on nomination of the secretary-general after consultation with governments. The original committee had five members from the West (the United Kingdom, France, Denmark, and Australia, plus the United States, which was represented by Carroll L. Wilson); three from the Eastern bloc (the USSR, Czechoslovakia, and Romania); three from Asia (Japan, India, and Pakistan); three from Africa (the United Arab Republic, Nigeria, and Mali); three from Latin America (Brazil, Argentina, Colombia); and one from the Middle East (Israel, represented by Abba Eban).

This committee certainly had enormous potential and, equally obviously, it could not be expected to produce spectacular results overnight. Broadly speaking, what was needed was both to improve the application in developing countries of the best knowledge already in existence and to identify especially important problems of new research or application deserving of priority attention. (Once such a problem *was* identified, what was going to be done about it? In an address before a New England audience, I let my imagination go: "The question arising after that will be one of will. If men can budget resources to go to the moon, can they budget them to de-salt the water of the sea economically . . . put electric energy where it will light the jungle village and take the heavy load off the villager's back . . . change the weather . . . end the rule of the tse-tse fly in that vast belt extending across Africa . . . wipe out protein deficiency throughout the world . . . muffle the population explosion?")

As de Seynes's special adviser on questions relating to science and technology, I served for nearly three years as secretary to the committee. Besides working closely with the committee as a whole, and its chairman (Nigerian biologist Eni Njoku, then M.S. Thacker from the Indian Planning Commission), and its other members individually, I also served as their connecting link with the various divisions at UN headquarters, with the four regional economic commissions, and, through a newly created coordinating committee, with the various specialized and other agencies in the UN system. This involved a good deal of travel, much of it to Europe.

It was an exhilarating job, and the committee made a successful start. Then, as far as I was concerned, a shadow began to darken the scene. All along I had been classified at the D-1 level and wanted to be promoted to D-2. I saw from the beginning—as everyone could well understand—that the higher grade was necessary to enable me to represent the committee with full effectiveness in all directions. In addition—although this was only my private concern—I personally needed the D-2 to let me be part of the select group that met from time to time, at dinner or otherwise, with high government officials including officials from Washington. Joining that group would enable me to talk with influential U.S. officials about my full-employment proposal. Experience showed that there was little use in writing letters; you had to *talk* with the people who could make things happen.

I was unable to get the raise I needed, although de Seynes tried to have me get it. Too many Americans had secured good positions with the UN at the beginning; there was no room left for late-comers. I agonized over this; declined an offer to stay on when I reached the official retirement age of sixty; and left the UN in March 1966.

My book *Insuring Full Employment,* subtitled *A United States Policy for Domestic Prosperity and World Development,* had been published by the Viking Press two years earlier. Senator Hubert Humphrey wrote the foreword. According to the dust jacket, "Without a general solution to the problem of unemployment, technological or otherwise, our economy (and our lives) cannot run smoothly. Mr. Pierson has devised just such a solution. His method is the operational method of science, and the breakthrough he has achieved lies in the separation of the economic problem of adequate demand from the political problem of how far to extend the operations of government."

The book received generally good reviews. Some brief excerpts: "I rate John H. G. Pierson's book among the best on the American economy in many a year" (Leon H. Keyserling in *The Progressive*). "Economically sound . . . a valuable contribution" (Garth L. Mangum in *Monthly Labor Review*). "A forcible argument. . . . Recommended for those interested in the economic and moral aspects of unemployment" (Louis E Buckley in *Ave Maria*). "An example of the best in economic writing" (Hirschel Kasper in *The Activist*). "An important and detailed diagnosis" (Crosby Forbes in *Boston Sunday Globe*). "A rewarding study based on humane considerations" (James V. Brown in *Library Journal*). "John Pierson exemplifies the fact that economics is not necessarily the dismal science" (William

U. Norwood, Jr., in *Annals of the American Academy of Political and Social Science*). "A mature and definitive statement by one of the great pioneers in the field of full employment" (Emile Benoit, my former colleague, now a professor in Columbia's Graduate School of Business). "No doubt Pierson's suggestion . . . will become the center of recurrent debate both in economic and political circles" (Gus Tyler, Assistant President, International Ladies' Garment Workers' Union).

Not everyone agreed. Some reviewers fastened narrowly on my proposal to guarantee overall consumer spending and said it would be ineffective, simply disregarding (like Hansen earlier) my further guarantee of the employment level itself and the crucial fact that the whole idea behind the consumer spending guarantee was to make that *employment* guarantee politically *possible*. Others complained that I ignored the basic maladjustments in society. Bernard Nossiter wrote in *Book Week* that, "The long and tortuous struggle to get a one-shot tax cut through Congress should teach Mr. Pierson and other equally well-intentioned economists that the problems of achieving full employment are deeply rooted in the nation's political and social structure. They involve questions of power, status and habit. Mechanical solutions based on narrow economic rationality are not good enough." I was considerably annoyed by Gerhard Colm's comments: "Pierson assumes that basic policies will promote a sound economic structure so that compensatory devices would only have to correct temporary deviations from a line moving in the right direction." I wrote to the National Planning Association, where Colm was the highly regarded chief economist and where I had had close connections in the past, calling them introverted and pretentious and asking them to stop sending me their reports. I was even more irritated by James F. Becker's complete distortions in his review for *The Nation*: Becker charged me with advocating pegging consumer spending "as high as possible" and "exorcising" public works and services. I wrote a lengthy rebuttal, which *The Nation* printed.

Most of the expressed objections seemed to stem from the fact that the objectors wanted more emphasis put on needed government programs. I certainly shared many of those liberal beliefs, and said so. As I wrote to Keyserling not long afterward, "Of course I agree with your view—or call it Galbraith's, for that matter—that we need more attention to the 'public sector'; I just don't want to make full employment play second fiddle even to that."

In May 1965 a *New York Times* editorial said that "Insurance against recession is needed, but both the nature and the timing of the President's fiscal dividend [Lyndon Johnson's heavy cuts in excise taxes] appear questionable." In a letter which the *Times* printed, I wrote that, "It seems time to stop juggling this (insurance against recession) as a phrase and instead establish it as a system." My letter went on to summarize again how that could be done.

Years later Charles Bolte, my editor at Viking, wrote to me about my proposal that "It continues to be persuasive to me. I only wonder why the policy-makers don't take it up."

8

Writing and Lobbying

In the old story from the *Arabian Nights,* Sindbad the sailor on one
of his voyages is shipwrecked on an island and encounters the Old
Man of the Sea. To accommodate this strange creature Sindbad car-
ries him across a stream on his shoulders, only to find that he cannot then put him down. Asked to descend, the Old Man simply twists
his legs tight around Sindbad's neck and beats him to drive him on.

Quite obviously I was Sindbad incarnate, and the cause of guaranteed full employment was my relentless Old Man of the Sea. In
1966 a request came from Alfred Jones, whom I thought of as almost
an older brother, to help write a book about the poverty problem for
his Foundation for Voluntary Service. The bad news at the time was
that 34 million Americans were counted as poor. Overcoming great
reluctance I composed a long chapter for a book that, as it turned out,
would never be completed.

Among the economic measures that my chapter approved were
negative income taxes (government *payments to* the poorest fami-

lies) and a guaranteed family income, but I qualified my support by saying that to guarantee income *before* guaranteeing the opportunity to work would be a mistake, creating "an odious new kind of class system in America. Those who had jobs could keep them if they liked; those who had not succeeded in obtaining jobs would of necessity form the core of the new leisure class. It is obvious that nobody wants this. . . ."

Automation was indeed threatening to make jobs ever harder to find, even though much needed work was just not being done. But the only tolerable ultimate answer to computers and robots, in my opinion, lay in sharing the work by reducing hours, not in condemning less competitive people to unemployment. "We don't need people as producers, we just need them as consumers," a leading advocate of guaranteed income had said. Who was the "we" in that sentence? "They also serve who only stand and consume." How could America agree to live by a dictum like that?

Meanwhile in A *"Freedom Budget" for All Americans,* a pamphlet put out by the A. Philip Randolph Institute, Leon Keyserling argued that poverty could be virtually abolished in America in the next ten years, without raising tax rates. His detailed analysis showed that attaining full employment would be by far the most important means to that end. Two hundred leaders of civil rights, religious, and labor groups had endorsed the proposed line of action. I wrote an article supporting it, too, but here again I deplored the tendency to speak too loosely of *guaranteeing.* "The guaranteeing of full employment is essential but not practicable by the means proposed in this pamphlet. But it would be practicable to guarantee full employment if one additional element [my guarantee of consumer spending] were added—and I hope that the sponsors of the 'Freedom Budget' can be persuaded of this."

In 1967, I sold my Connecticut house and moved to Honolulu. I was to move back to Connecticut six years later, but in the meantime, from my office near Diamond Head I launched an intensive writing campaign. Some two dozen articles would be drafted in the next ten years (and for the most part brought together in another book, *Essays on Full Employment, 1942–1972**). Letters enclosing my latest pieces would be mailed out by the score. Letters to governors and mayors, labor leaders and businessmen, fellow economists, educators, churchmen. Letters to the heads of nonprofit organizations, including John W. Gardner of Common Cause and Ralph Nader of Public Citizen (I entertained some hope that one or both of them would take up my proposal), as well as the League of Women Voters, environmentalists, and others. Letters to newspaper reporters, columnists, editors, publishers, TV commentators, and other media people were sent as well. Occasionally I managed to get radio or television time to state my case. I would say, for instance, that expecting the device of "government as employer of last resort" to guarantee full employment all by itself, without help from a real *assurance* of adequate demand, was like asking a bird to fly on one wing. I continued to write to prominent public figures in many fields. Sometimes I felt that by repeatedly sounding this call for action I was inflicting a sort of Chinese water torture on my correspondents. Most of all, I sent letters to government officials and to congressmen in Washington.

Getting published was a perennial problem. One of my worst disappointments came with an article, later published in the *Honolulu Advertiser,* that I first submitted as a letter to the editor of the *Groton School Quarterly.* "The problems that by their and our very nature hold our attention," this piece began, "are not economic (technical)—they are social (human and moral): how to preserve our planet and live in decent friendship and cooperation with our fellow men of every age, race, and creed. . . . Nevertheless, we have to solve the problem of economic performance—which we are obviously failing to do at this time—in order to gain even the chance to

---

*(Metuchen, N.J.: Scarecrow Press, 1972).

solve some of our most pressing social problems. We have no choice but to attend to the economic foundations of our social structure." This seemed to me an appropriate message to Groton's disproportionately influential alumni, and I badly needed support from some of them. It was ironical that a school where "service to church and state" had been dinned into me as a student, a school that had even honored me by declaring a general holiday at the time of my rather spectacular graduation from Yale, would not print this piece or even explain why. The *Quarterly*'s editor did in a subsequent issue invite those interested in my views to get in touch with me about them, but that was too little and too late to undo the damage.

Washington was tolerably within range because I could make stopovers there on my way to and from the Greek afforestation project I had begun spending time on in 1964. I wrote a somewhat hilarious book about the struggles my son and I went through to buy the land for that project. I became seriously interested, too, in old Eastern and contemporary Western thought about the power of the mind to influence the body, going so far as to write a short book about Zen as interpreted by the living French physician Hubert Benoit. I joined a World Order Program group at the University of Hawaii and helped publicize the proposed International Law of the Sea convention. To keep healthy I jogged, slept, and swam.

I wasted no time in bringing my proposal for economic performance insurance to the attention of Hawaii's political leaders. Even before actually moving to the islands I was invited to deliver an address at their Governor's Conference on Human Services in Honolulu. "I have two quite simple propositions that I want to make," I began. "The first is that we ought to guarantee full employment in the United States. And the second is that it can be done."

Governor John A. Burns called the concept fascinating. Soon afterward I had appointments in Washington with Hawaii's four members of Congress. Democratic Senator Daniel Inouye told me that he liked my pragmatic approach, and gave me letters of introduction to a number of other Senators. "Needless to say," Inouye wrote later, "I agree with your basic premise that we have to solve the problem of economic performance before we have any chance of solving many of the other pressing human problems." Republican Senator Hiram Fong asked me to write him a letter, which he would then send to President Nixon. Actually, however, he sent it only to Paul Mc-Cracken, chairman of Nixon's Council of Economic Advisers, with whom I was already in touch. Democratic Representative (later, Senator) Spark Matsunaga, active in promoting progressive legislation, commended me on my "eloquent and persuasive" advocacy of full employment. Matsunaga agreed to explore with Inouye my suggestion that the keynote address at the 1968 Democratic Convention should commit the party to assuring everyone in America the chance to work. (The platform on which Hubert Humphrey ran unsuccessfully that year did in fact offer a full-employment pledge—"For those who cannot obtain other employment, the federal government will be the employer of last resort"—and similar language would appear in Democratic platforms at regular intervals thereafter. The trouble with all such "commitments," however, was that, lacking the further guarantee of an adequate level of demand for private production output, they implied the possibility of "creeping socialism," or at any rate of having to fill gaps with more public sector employment than was either feasible or wanted, and so they could never be taken seriously or actually carried out.) Democratic Representative Patsy Mink discussed tactics with me—above all the need to find a prominent political figure to spearhead my campaign—and in 1972 she put into the *Congressional Record* one of my most important articles, "Completing the Employment Act," which contained my suggestions for the necessary new legislative text.

There was nothing partisan in the political sense about my proposal. Progressive Republicans in the House had formed a "Wednesday Group," chaired by Charles Whalen (Ohio). At the request of the group's staff director, Sven Groennings, I wrote a paper explaining my idea. Its status was reported back as "alive but not very lively," especially in view of the imminent 1970 Congressional elections. When Groennings moved from Capitol Hill to the State Department near the end of that year, this project lapsed.

Among the other senators whom I met, thanks to Inouye's help, were Jacob Javits (New York), William Proxmire (Wisconsin), Fred Harris (Oklahoma), and Harold Hughes (Iowa), all of them deeply concerned with the unemployment problem. The reception I got from them was in general very good—as it was from former Senator Paul Douglas (Illinois) and Representative Henry Reuss (Wisconsin). They made me more fully aware, however, of the widely prevalent view that full employment would bring inflation with it, as the popular "trade-off" theory had it, and also aware of the skepticism over whether Congress would ever give up any of its cherished prerogatives to shift some power to the executive branch.

This last concern, I insisted, was based on a misconception. Congress would *not* under EPI give up any prerogatives worth mentioning; it would gain new control instead. For it was Congress that would set the policies on the levels of employment and consumer spending to be maintained, and would choose the compensatory measures to be brought into play by the President whenever those policies would otherwise not be enforced. All that Congress would let go of in exchange would be its divisive, ineffective, and time-consuming moment-by-moment attempts at economic backseat driving.

Fear of inflation, on the other hand, certainly did provide legitimate grounds for caution, and I had to keep explaining why my EPI policy would help to control inflation rather than cause it. I concentrated on that in "Best Cure for Inflation—Guaranteed Full Employment," an article published in *The Commercial and Financial Chronicle* in 1969. My argument there and in my other papers came down to this: (1) The ceilings that EPI would place over total consumer spending (along with the floors put under it) would effectively prevent excessive demand pull and limit the need for cost-of-living wage boosts. (2) Production costs would be held down for two additional reasons: full employment spreads overhead costs over more units of output; and elimination of business cycles would minimize the need for business and labor to cushion anticipated recessions with special business reserves and job-security clauses in union contracts. (3) Although business and labor shy away from acting "responsibly" on prices and wages as long as government fails to accept *its* responsibility for maintaining a prosperous full-employment economy, that attitude could be expected to change once government *did* accept *its* responsibility and the general public knew what the new situation was. (4) *The expectation of inflation,* historically a major cause of *current* inflation, would virtually disappear. Shortages of nonrenewable resources such as oil could still push certain prices upward if substitutes were not found, but full employment could not reasonably be blamed for that.

In 1970 Henry Reuss and others were calling for a "quick freeze" to halt the rise of prices and wages, and President Nixon did in fact impose that temporary restraint a year later. Economist John Kenneth Galbraith, going farther, maintained that *permanent* wage and price controls were essential. In one of several articles I wrote for the *Honolulu Advertiser* that year, I conceded that Galbraith might be right. "Certainly this cannot be disproved as of now. But it cannot be proved yet either. Before we treat it as if it could be, I suggest that we first try a different approach: a 'quick freeze' now, then the offer of a firm guarantee of full employment, in exchange for which business and labor leaders should agree to abide by some reasonable set of price and wage guidelines."

At about that time the *New York Times* devoted most of its "Op-Ed" page—a feature recently established by Harrison Salisbury—to three articles about wages and prices. The first, by Leonard Woodcock, argued that "Wage Increases Don't Cause Inflationary Spirals." The second, by John A. Davenport, said "To Combat Inflation Union Monopoly Power Must Be Curbed." The final one, which I wrote, ran under the heading "A Comprehensive Plan to Balance Our Economic Life"—upgraded by Salisbury from my more modest title, "Full Employment Need Not Generate Inflation."

In 1970, I ran a series of six articles in the *Monterey Peninsula Herald*. I also had a personal letter of introduction to the influential chairman of the House Ways and Means Committee, Wilbur Mills (Arkansas). Mills treated me with exemplary courtesy and referred me to Lawrence Woodworth, chief of staff of the Joint Committee on Internal Revenue Taxation. The talks with Woodworth and four of his economists went well, judging by what I was told about Woodworth's report to Mills. The pressure of other legislative business, however, kept a plan for follow-up discussions from being carried out.

I also set out to try to convince Senator Edmund Muskie (Maine). After having inconclusive talks with several other staff members, I was referred to Muskie's economist, Richard Richardson. This made a good discussion possible and, convinced further by reading some of my papers, Richardson reported very favorably on my proposal to Senator Muskie. My "big" idea fitted in, I was told; it should not be passed by. That, however, was as far as things got. Muskie's campaign for the presidency was handled mainly by lawyers; Richardson left Washington in some frustration to become Director of Research at the Twentieth Century Fund; and my subsequent correspondence with the senator and his staff amounted to little more than a formality.

"The candidates are setting their economic sights too low," I wrote in the *Washington Post* in the spring of 1972. "Sen. Edmund Muskie has said: 'It is time to commit our nation to the right to a job.' Sen. George McGovern: 'If I were President of the United States, I would set as the first order of business the creation of a decent job for every American.' Sen. Henry Jackson: 'As far as I am concerned, the Employment Act of 1946 means what it says . . . that the Federal Government under any administration, Republican or Democratic, must be prepared to use all the powers at its command to see that people have work.' Sen. Hubert Humphrey: 'Employment is a right for every American, like freedom or due process. Government has an obligation to fulfill that right as the first matter of policy.' . . . But [I commented] without an explanation of how it can be accomplished this does little more than widen the credibility gap."

For a moment that year it seemed that I might be close to a breakthrough. In my approach to Senator Walter Mondale (Minnesota), I made a convert of Herbert Jasper, Mondale's assistant on the Labor and Public Welfare Committee. Jasper in turn enlisted key staff members of Senators Alan Cranston (California) and Gaylord Nelson (Wisconsin). A quick check with economists Arthur Okun and Walter Heller and with the executive director and the chief economist of the Joint Economic Committee raised no serious problems. The intended next step was for a letter to be sent by the three senators to a number of the "high priests" of economics saying that something like what I proposed had to be done and asking for their specific reaction. After that, and a hearing before the Joint Economic Committee, a bill would be introduced. Before any of this could happen, however, Senator Javits introduced a bill of his own along similar if less conclusive lines, and my initiative was derailed. (A few years later I was to circulate rather widely in Washington a memorandum saying that I admired Walter Heller and Arthur Okun but that, in the absence of economic performance insurance, their brand of economics was limited in what it could accomplish. "Good economic advisers are not enough without a definite, recurring legislative procedure. Such a procedure is not enough without well-selected targets. Those targets are not enough unless they are firm. Firmness is impossible without contingent arrangements." This referred of course to the actions that would be taken under EPI *if and only if* they were shown to be needed to meet the guarantees.)

I moved back to Connecticut, closer to Washington, D.C., and continued my efforts. To Paul Simon (Illinois), whose successful run for the House in 1974 stressed the need for a full-employment economy, I wrote (enclosing a campaign contribution) that " I hope you will get elected. Then I hope you will really do something about this great issue—to which so many politicians have given so much lip service." In a series of letters responding to articles I sent to him, Simon thanked me for my "pioneering," appreciated my "continued leadership," was pleased to be "on the same wave length," and said, "You make a great deal of sense to me." But this ended when Simon decided to advocate a Constitutional amendment mandating a balanced budget. "While I agree with you," he wrote in 1977, "that provisions of Humphrey-Hawkins should be meshed with the new budget process, I have doubts whether it would be wise to allow contingent spending." Congressional authorization of spending on a contingent basis—i.e., if needed to enforce *Congressionally established* employment and consumer spending guarantees—was, of course, at the heart of my proposal. (Ten years later, Paul Simon as senator and presidential contender published a hard-hitting book titled *Let's Put America Back to Work.* The centerpiece of his plan was a substantially improved version of the New Deal's WPA. I wrote a review, which I failed to get published, praising the book's strong points but pointing out the impracticality of actually guaranteeing job opportunities for all—as the dust jacket implied—unless the level of market demand would be guaranteed, too. "Is it possible for you to see my proposal as the logical extension of your own ideas?" I asked Simon, enclosing a copy of my review. There was no reply.)

Missouri Democrat Richard Bolling, one of the dominant figures in the House, saw clearly both the economic value of EPI and the political difficulty of getting it enacted into law. "No doubt your early systematic discussion," he wrote me, "has influenced my thinking since I first found it in one of your essays or books." There were talks in Bolling's office. I wrote to Bolling at length with suggestions for text amendments on a 1975 legislative draft. The following year Bolling inserted an article of mine in the *Congressional Record.* Another insert in the *Record* followed almost immediately, this one a long letter to Senator Abraham Ribicoff (Connecticut) explaining why full employment need not cause inflation. (Unfortunately for me, Bolling decided to retire from Congress in 1982.)

While doing my best to get something started in Washington, I also played to the hinterland. In 1975, I wrote a paper for one of the Democratic town committees in Connecticut on "How to Get Economic Performance Insurance Started Now." The following year I circulated a brief note, "In the Spirit of '76," as part of an exploration of the feasibility of establishing a Center for a National Full-Employment Policy. The year after that I circulated another paper, "For a New Start," saying in conclusion: "The real question is whether a political movement can take shape to get that policy [guaranteed full employment] established. I hope that President Carter with the support of like-minded members of Congress from both parties will see to that. If not, then somebody else should take the lead. But first there needs to be publicity. Nothing gets done nowadays without publicity. So I ask this question: Who is going to provide the publicity for a drive to give America guaranteed full employment without inflation?" Also in 1977, I mailed out some seventy-five copies of "A Request for Discussion," mainly to newswriters and other publicists, asking that they examine the guaranteed full-employment proposal and analyze it in their columns. "Details have been circulated quite widely in Washington, in Congress and the administration, and will be gladly mailed to you on request."

The response to these several initiatives was negligible, as was—on the surface, at least—the gain to me from the many letters I received from Washington thanking me for "taking the time to share my thoughts." Nevertheless I felt that even here I was often building latent understanding and support that would become overt once someone else, some political leader, decided that it was time to come out openly for the EPI plan. On the other hand, what really bothered me was to be condescended to or be thanked for my appreciation of what some official was doing when in fact I had tried to suggest what that official could be doing but wasn't. My anger sometimes got the better of me then. For example, in January 1978, I responded at some length to a circulated letter from Jimmy Carter which contained an invitation to share any thoughts about important issues on the American agenda. Secretary of Labor Ray Marshall answered me on behalf of the President. "I know you agree with me," he wrote, "that [unemployment] is one of the important problems that the country is currently facing." Bristling, I wrote back: "Dear Mr. Secretary: One thing that you people certainly do learn to do down there in Washington is to write a truly insulting letter. . . ."

What dominated the scene in those years, however, was the memorable Humphrey-Hawkins attempt to improve on the Employment Act of 1946. I was left out of it; my Washington contacts just were not good enough to get me in on this action in time to influence its course. When I first heard about this proposed legislation in 1974, I immediately asked for an opportunity to testify at hearings on it. Neither then, however, when ideas about its text were still fluid, nor later when further tinkering with an already widely accepted text might have slowed the bill's momentum, was I given that opportunity. Augustus E. Hawkins (California), chairman of the House Subcommittee on Employment Opportunities, asked me instead to submit my comments in written form. This I did, elaborating on a note I had already sent to the bill's numerous sponsors and co-sponsors and to members of the Joint Economic Committee.

"There is no doubt that the Humphrey-Hawkins bill would be much stronger if it contained the amendments which you suggest," Leon Keyserling, the bill's main author, wrote to me. "Your proposals may well make this Act a better piece of legislation," wrote Senator Humphrey. "I have, of course, greatly admired your work as an innovator of ideas."

"I am committed to the concept of the Humphrey-Hawkins bill in its present form," wrote Morris K. Udall (Arizona), whose candidacy for President I had been supporting. "While minor amendments may be adopted, I do not believe that it would be helpful to introduce into the record plans outlining major changes in the bill. This is a very controversial piece of legislation and a tremendous amount of work will be required to enact it into law." I had indeed missed the boat.

As enacted, the Full Employment and Balanced Growth [Humphrey-Hawkins] Act of 1978 set a goal of not more than three percent adult unemployment, to be attained within four years. It also spelled out at length the policies and procedures to be followed with that goal in mind—planning and general economic policies; countercyclical, structural, and youth employment policies; policies and procedures for Congressional review; etc. My written testimony endorsed the bill (needlessly cumbersome though I felt it to be) but argued for amendments to strengthen it. First and foremost, it needed clarification of the text to indicate unmistakably that full employment was not just a goal ("it has been a goal for a long time!") but a promise, and a number of other language changes, along EPI lines. Second, it needed some language to make sure that another new law, the Congressional Budget Act, would not prevent authorization of contingent actions in support of employment and consumer spending if required to honor the promises in Humphrey-Hawkins once they were given. Third, it needed a rewording of the section concerned with Congressional review of the annual plans, to make clear that the whole exercise must arrive at definite, action-shaping conclusions on the essential points.

A great many forward-looking Americans invested a lot of time, energy, and hope in the struggle for Humphrey-Hawkins. As far as solving the unemployment problem was concerned, it became a dead letter almost as soon as it was enacted.

9

Widening the Campaign

Why had I not been more successful in my battle so far? The main reason seemed to me to be that my idea was new. Ideas of any kind that are new or different meet with psychological resistance, unless it is clear that there is money to be made out of them. Whenever a major new idea cannot easily be attacked directly, it is resisted by being ignored. Even the inventor of the wheel must have been given a hard time. Why roll things? What's wrong with dragging them or shoving them, the way we've always done?

If Representative Jonathan Bingham (New York) was right, the period of nonrecognition need not last forever. "I feel that somehow, sometime this country will have to move the way John Pierson points," he wrote in 1980 to the publisher of my newest book. But *somehow, sometime*! Congress, at least, was not going to be in a hurry over anything so newfangled!

The novelty of my idea was of course not the only problem. Some people—a minority but by no means a negligible number—would be *against* it automatically. Included were those employers who wanted unemployment to be *high* to help them hold down wages, and probably also those financial traders who specialized in playing the cyclical swings rather than the best buys. And *what* special interest group could be expected to campaign *for* it—for something the benefits of which would accrue to practically everyone without discrimination? Even organized labor, although certainly very much in favor of full employment, was more concerned over the wages and working conditions of union members than over making sure that all of the involuntarily unemployed got jobs. Finally, sad to say, among politicians there always seemed to be some who managed to subordinate their interest in solving the unemployment problem to their partisan desire to blame the other political party for not solving it.

I also realized that I could expect most professional economists to stay pretty much on the sidelines when it came to judging my plan. Not a very large number were working seriously on the central questions of national economic policy; far more made a living by teaching survey courses or some economic specialty, or by helping their corporate employer maximize profits, or by forecasting. And as for those who actually did concentrate on "political economy," many had an evident bias in favor of some particular interest (business, agriculture, labor, etc.), so that their opinions were apt to be slanted.

Economists without any such bias were obviously the ones whose support I especially wanted to have—and did have in some cases, as already noted. Outright endorsement was not easy to come by, however, from someone who had a nationwide reputation for prudence and sagacity to defend. Paul Samuelson, for example, long at the top of his profession, wrote to a friend of mine, Bryn Beorse, that he certainly would not criticize my proposal, but neither was he ready to make it his. I could only conclude that Paul, for all his brilliance, had not thought deeply enough about the pivotal importance of job opportunity in its relation to all the other interacting variables economists have to deal with.

I did risk giving a certain amount of offense with my irreverent attitude toward economic theory. "The conflicting views of distinguished experts about how to promote prosperity can only generate a certain agnosticism about economic theories," I wrote in *Insuring Full Employment.* "This lack of dedication to a theory, however, could become a comparatively harmless affliction. For example, with aggregate consumer spending insured . . . our ability to maintain the effective demand needed for full employment would not depend on commitment to a theory of oversaving, a theory of undersaving, or any other."

My main concern in the matter of economic theory, however, was to have it understood that EPI was not itself a *conflicting* doctrine. Ideological conflicts were inevitable (between Keynesians and supply-siders, for example), but EPI would hold a protective "umbrella" over them. There were few real differences of opinion, I thought, between me and my fellow economists with a working interest in the same objectives. One such issue did arise, however, whenever someone thought "that my proposal is against, or perhaps disregards the importance of, his or her proposal. That is a misconception in principle. EPI is an umbrella policy, potentially consistent with any and all other measures, be they 'liberal' or 'conservative,' for promoting prosperity and stability at the full-employment level."* In other words, those other measures would continue to yield better or worse first approximations of the results intended, and actual attainment of those results would be assured through the EPI standby adjustments agreed upon in advance. ("My private views on the kinds of other measures our country needs have been indicated repeatedly, of course. . . ." Actually, the limited space allowed for articles caused me usually to omit any mention of those other needed measures, and this then sometimes created misunderstandings.)

I went into the 1980s with pretty much the same strategy as be-

---

*From the preface to my *Full Employment without Inflation* (1980).

fore. I wrote articles—mainly for newspapers, to shorten the time-lag—and sent copies to people who might be in a position to influence events (administration officials, candidates for nomination for president, members of Congress, newspaper columnists, governors of states and mayors of large cities, other prominent individuals). I was considerably encouraged by the fact that many of their replies expressed genuine appreciation. Both Walter Mondale and Michael Dukakis during their runs for the presidency showed some interest. But nobody went so far as to offer to take action. I also failed in a brief attempt to get a foundation grant or other financial support for publicizing my proposal more widely.

My fifth book on the subject, *Full Employment without Inflation* with the subtitle *Papers on the Economic Performance Insurance (EPI) Proposal,* was published in 1980 by Allenheld, Osmun & Co. The wife of the publisher-editor said at the last minute that she couldn't see why I hadn't written up my idea just once instead of saying the same thing so many times over! The book opened with "The Importance and Practicality of Guaranteed Full Employment," a lengthy article which had appeared in abridged form in the summer 1979 issue of *Journal of Post Keynesian Economics.* "In sum," I wrote there, "the inadequacy of our basic economic policies keeps us collectively poorer than we need to be, exaggerates the welfare burden, reinforces discrimination against women and minorities, destroys the self-reliant character of millions of Americans by showing them that their contributions are unwanted, pits interest groups too hard against society as a whole, and undermines foreign relations, especially with the Third World. This is a course that needs to be reversed before it brings us to disaster."

Toward the end of this piece, for which I received a large number of favorable reactions, I included a thumbnail historical sketch: "The Classical School held that there was an inherent tendency toward full employment, since supply *was* demand. Keynes found that that was not so, but concluded 'that a somewhat comprehensive socialization of investment will prove the only means of securing an approximation of full employment.' In America, Hansen leaned toward the related view that the way to take up economic slack was to expand public investment. Others soon emphasized that slack can be taken up equally well by additional private spending, from tax reduction. So far, so good. But then somehow the pursuit of full employment got lost amid the loud claims of those who *wanted* tax reduction and *opposed* government spending, or the reverse. No doubt this helps to explain why many economists became disenchanted with fiscal policy. Under EPI, however, the tendency toward full employment would be deliberately restored and reinforced, those rival claims notwithstanding."

In "Cut the Economic Gordian Knot," one of several articles I had published in local Connecticut newspapers in 1983, I wrote that we certainly cannot get permanent full employment "from any known liberal Democratic formula or from a conservative Republican one—from Keynes or monetarism or supply-side economics or any other special and hence limited approach. Instead we have to get it by adopting a new, essentially general 'insurance' approach—not special and limited, not a speculative remedy at all—and by keeping that policy in effect all the time, above politics, let the liberal-conservative tide on other issues swing as it may. . . . We have multiple objectives and—in our world of side effects, conflicts, and chance— the solution of the pivotal problem gets lost for lack of a special device to make sure that it doesn't get lost. Any claim that full employment can be won and kept as the by-product of something else (an expanded welfare package, for instance, or by taking the shackles off business) is false or simply naive. Here is an intricate knot that cannot be untied but has to be cut. Yet it can be cut by adopting an 'insurance' approach that takes the final results of all the moves and crosscurrents into account."

This article, too, was quite widely applauded, and it got some attention from abroad as well. Guy Gresford, former executive director of the Commonwealth Scientific and Industrial Research Organization (CSIRO), who had succeeded me in the UN science and technology post, wrote me that, "Your diagnosis of the U.S. problem would apply, word for word, I think, to the Australian situation." Leonora Stettner, a colleague of mine forty years earlier in the Postwar Division of BLS, wrote from London that, "Your thesis is of vital importance. . . . Written for the U.S. context, it is equally applicable to our desperate situation here. . . . I am convinced that one of these decades the full employment guarantee will be accepted as too obvious to require comment." Actually, I had insisted from the beginning that I was not presuming to prescribe for any country other than the United States. However, in a letter to the editor of the *International Herald Tribune* in 1978 I did say that studies might show the applicability of EPI to some other countries as well. (Indeed, it could ultimately become the universal economic system for all advanced economies. Right, left, or center, one could imagine all of them following the EPI plan, differing only in the preferred size of their public sector.)

Leonora Stettner, an American economist with wide experience who was now assisting Lord Oram in the British House of Lords, was a gifted writer and editor. Her letter gave me the inspiration for a possible new way to broaden my campaign. Could she find time to write a book about my proposal, drawing on my books and articles for raw material? To my immense gratification, she wrote that she could. What emerged in due course, after several trans-Atlantic trips on her part, was a remarkably well-organized and annotated short paperback book, *Guaranteed Full Employment: A Proposal for Achieving Continuous Work Opportunity for All, Without Inflation, Through "Economic Performance Insurance" (EPI)*, "Selected and Edited from the Writings of John H. G. Pierson by Leonora Stettner."

"What is different and additional about [Pierson's] proposal," Stettner wrote in her preface, "is his stress on the role of *expectations* in the economy, and hence on the possibility, as well as the need, for creating an insurance mechanism to *guarantee* a full-employment level of economic activity. It is not good enough, he argues, for governments merely to exert their 'best efforts' to minimize unemployment. Because of the many hazards blocking the path of good intentions . . . something more than pious hopes and unsecured promises is required to engender the kind of expectations that will *sustain* a full-employment level of activity. Investors, managers, trade unions and customers cannot be relied on to make expansionary decisions unless they are truly confident of the markets, or job opportunities, or incomes which will in the end justify such decisions."

Published in the United States in 1985 by the North River Press, this booklet was mailed to about five thousand persons on a list I prepared—some three thousand of the American Economic Association's members; nearly a thousand people in government (mayors and city managers, governors of states, Reagan administration members, members of the relevant Senate and House committees); and another thousand altogether of newspaper and magazine editors, college presidents, religious leaders, trade union research directors, heads of state chambers of commerce, heads of other membership organizations, influential individuals not in any of those categories, and personal friends.

The response in reviews and correspondence was rather meager but gratifying as far as it went. An unexpected by-product was a debate on employment policy that took place in the House of Lords early the following year, with Lord Oram and several other members discussing the possible applicability of my proposal to Great Britain. The views expressed were more favorable than not, but subsequently a British critic said that I was a crank. The word sent a shudder through me when I heard of it, as it happened to be one that my father had sometimes used as an ultimate sort of disparagement of someone or other long years before. Could it be that the old joke, "I turned out to be the kind of man my father warned me against," was directly applicable to me?

This was not an altogether fanciful notion. I was having personal trouble with the fact that I cared as much as I did about my great idea. It possessed me. It brought me no really significant amount of public discussion, and at the same time made me feel stupid in private social life. I could not talk about it any more with friends, and could hardly keep up with their talk about other subjects. The loneliness of it was not easy for me to bear. To preserve some semblance of harmony at home I was beginning to promise that after the effort I was currently making I was finally going to stop, only to find out later that I was unable to keep that promise. My battle wounds ached. I even had the heart-breaking experience of losing the moral support of my one-time working colleague and longtime close friend, Alfred Jones. Alfred, who had once called EPI an idea whose time had come, now said that it was an idea whose time "has come and gone." I could only hope that Alfred's judgment had been warped by too-long daily exposure to short-term stock market trends. It came down to having to hope that my own continuing gut feeling and intellectual conviction about the practicality and importance of EPI were not an illusion. I was as expendable as anyone else, no quarrel with that, but, surely, to be expended for *nothing* would be the ultimate loss.

In 1985 Ted Turner founded the Better World Society to bring television to bear on "the three key problems that threaten life on our planet: nuclear arms, a burgeoning world population, and the degradation of our environment." I asked to have the full-employment issue taken into account in the BWS program, too. Efforts to accelerate disarmament and to stop the ruination of the environment would both win political support more easily, I argued, if EPI were in place to insure against adverse economic consequences. Nothing came of this initiative, but the argument linking those issues was timely and it continued to play a prominent part in my campaign after that. "Economic performance insurance is a plan for ending the classic fear of a shortage of markets," I wrote in the article whose rejection by the *Washington Post* staggered me in 1989. "Surely America should lead the way in a world looking to escape disaster from its weapons and the abused environment. . . . Why wait? A risk of recession is no good reason. Recession can be avoided even during rapid change. Dispensed with for good and all too."

I tried without success to have this theme developed by *other* writers, asking the editor of the *New Haven Register* and other newspapers to consider doing a series of articles on these issues and their interconnections. I also appealed to Denis Hayes, Jim Maddy, Lester Brown, Peter Bahouth, Fred Krupp, and other prominent environmentalists to recognize how much their movement would gain if the fear of conflict between environmentalism and economics were removed. In return I unexpectedly found myself put on the National Environmental Leadership Council, but I still didn't get much understanding of the argument I was trying to make. As for the disarmament aspect, when I tried to explain this to the Reverend William Sloane Coffin, President of SANE/FREEZE, Coffin first told me I was "right on the money" but later changed to saying that "to improve the economy as it now works would be to hurt both the environment and poor people even more."

I could make little sense of this. Could this turnaround have been based on some sort of misunderstanding of the views of Coffin's chief associate, Seymour Melman, who was chairman of the National Commission for Economic Conversion and Disarmament? Ten years earlier Melman had written me that I was right about full-employment policy on theoretical grounds but that it was necessary for reasons of practicality to focus on the politically workable issue of economic conversion from military industry. For my part I could see no conflict between these issues. As I put it in that same vexed 1989 article, "If we just shut our arms plants down, demobilize troops, ban all toxic substances, and force production costs up with stiff antipollution measures, then obviously the resulting layoffs of workers and loss of income could easily start a downward spiral. But that simply will not happen if two steps are taken to prevent [it]. Step one: do some detailed swords-into-plowshares planning for a transition period. The National Commission for Economic Conversion and Disarmament has been studying this aspect. Step two: adopt a policy of 'economic performance insurance' as immediate bottom-line support and as the basis for permanent prosperity when conversion planning is no longer relevant."

My best approach to the Bush administration seemed to me to be through valedictorian and Rhodes scholar Roger B. Porter, who had served both Ford and Reagan and was now assistant to the president for Economic and Domestic Policy. When the *New York Times* in early 1989 quoted Bush as saying that changes in the coming decade would "shift attention away from worries about the supply of jobs that have haunted us since the 1930s and toward new concerns about the supply of workers and skills," I wrote again to Porter, saying that such statements seemed misleading and unfortunate. (1) The risk of running short of skilled workers should not be used to obscure the need to provide work opportunity for the larger number who are less skilled. (2) Our unemployment statistics do not by any means show that nearly all Americans now have the opportunity to work. (3) The argument that demographic trends foreshadow a *shortage* of workers completely overlooks one of the major forces now loose in the world—the incoming tide of workers from a world population growth not yet under control. (4) There is the great danger that, out of fear of recession and higher unemployment, America will move too slowly on disarmament and on saving the environment. Another presidential assistant answered for Porter, saying simply that the administration had always been committed to the pursuit of economic policies that would increase jobs, investment, and economic growth.

I made an effort to persuade Connecticut's members of Congress to join together, regardless of party, in introducing effective full-employment legislation. About all that I had to show, however, for this and for other efforts with Washington representatives of my home state was some essentially noncommittal letters from my senators.

One from Christopher Dodd said that, "I certainly continue to be intrigued by your theory, which reflects a high level of scholarship. While such ideas may seem radical in times of economic expansion, I am sure that many Connecticut residents who are currently unemployed would have a particular insight as to why such a scheme might work." From Joseph Lieberman: "I was certainly pleased and surprised at your suggestions for attaining full employment here in the United States. I have heard many discussions on how we can come close to this, but this is the first comparatively concrete idea I have seen on attaining work for all able-bodied workers." Connecticut Senator Brien McMahon had been less cautious in his support fifty years earlier.

In 1991, I wrote an article on also putting an end to *job discrimination.* "The civil rights bill struggle proves again," I began, "that America needs a surefire way of having enough jobs to go around. Affirmative steps are essential to help remedy past discrimination, yet how could a white worker not resent losing a job to a less qualified worker who happened to be black or Hispanic? Who *ought* to get the scarce jobs? The dilemma is obvious. The solution lies in adopting a procedure to keep the number of jobs in line with the number of men and women able and seeking to work."

The *Greenwich Time* accepted this piece out of hand but then printed it under my name in such emasculated form that I would have been ashamed to have written what the reader saw.

The following year I was invited to contribute to a collection of essays in *Buying America Back,* edited by Jonathan Greenberg and William Kistler and published by Council Oak Books of Tulsa, Oklahoma. The book never sold particularly well but I reprinted my own contribution, "Insuring Prosperous Times and Full Employment," and mailed it to all members of the incoming Congress. Emphasizing that a permanent full-employment policy would still be needed when recovery from the present recession was finally achieved, I asked that my proposal be considered as a basis for legislative action. Several dozen members replied, some of them out of courtesy, others clearly impressed.

In the course of dealing one more time with various facets of my proposal, I wrote at some length in this article about what EPI would *cost* if it were adopted:

> To worry about the cost of EPI might seem almost laughable after all the budget deficits we have incurred for weapons and for salvaging people and corporations struck down by recessions. Still, "can we afford it?" is a question that calls for a serious answer in terms of the federal budget and in real cost/benefit terms also.
>
> In real terms the costs would be quite minor and the benefits major to say the least. Benefits would include elimination of the "nonproduction" that results from unemployment; considerable substitution of "butter" for "guns," since disarmament could be speeded up without overall economic risk; somewhat better allocation of resources, from greater ability to relax trade barriers; meaningful additions to quality of life from faster adoption of key environmental reforms; reduction of the misery of enforced idleness and of the social ills stemming from that. As for costs, the EPI system would require a certain amount of new governmental apparatus for maintaining and operating the nationwide reserve shelf of public works and services. This could occur with no net increase in the size of government, however, if people were simultaneously released from those parts of government currently providing services related to unemployment. Also, much of the likely expansion of job training and placement services would fall within the private sector.
>
> In strictly financial (government budget) terms, it seems difficult to say whether the aggregate benefits would generally exceed or generally fall short of the aggregate costs. Our welfare costs—in the widest sense, with extended unemployment compensation included—could be greatly reduced. There would also, in the longer run, be more taxpaying ability from a more productive population. On the other hand, the ability of presumptively ad-

equate consumer spending to sustain full employment might be impaired by corporations which raise prices and restrict output, for example [or, the latest problem, engage in wholesale downsizing]; or by excessive government regulation. Similarly, the ability of full employment to sustain adequate consumer spending might be impaired by too uneven income distribution or (as almost certainly today) by the "leakage" from spending at home that results from our foreign trade deficit. Far from *causing* such difficulties, however, the EPI system would not merely compensate for them but would help identify their origins and so [over time, in a beneficial feedback effect] make remedies easier to apply.

I ended this, my last essay, as follows: "We are in a long pause between the historic New Deal discovery that depressions aren't acts of God and the awareness that serious business-cycle and unemployment problems can be eliminated altogether. The knowledge we now have, and the challenges we face, demand that we bring that pause to an end."

10

Conclusions

Near the beginning of my long crusade, I had paid at least passing attention to the problems bedeviling innovation in general. Not that I doubted the eventual success of my own campaign. We have all seen it happen, I wrote. At first people say no, it can't be done. Later on, of course, it is done, and then they say, oh well, the thing is obvious, anybody could have seen it, there's nothing to it. Looking back some sixty years later, in a time of rising demand for change one way or another, I still think that events may ultimately justify the optimism I felt then.

Heart and head both tell us, I believe, that securing permanent full employment in America should be a next step. It is needed and it can be had. The indignity and physical suffering of the jobless themselves do not have to continue. Discrimination against women and minorities can virtually disappear. Our national income will automatically rise as "nonproduction" declines. The burden on society of fighting drugs and crime, closely linked as it certainly is with unemployment, can be substantially lightened. So can the heavy cost of welfare programs of all kinds, without loss of compassion; effective welfare reform is not just a matter of forcing people too long on welfare to go to work; the other side of the coin is a policy that makes sure that the jobs they need are really available. So, too, can be lightened the extra expense passed on to us all by business and labor in their present need to cushion themselves against recessions expected in future; and the compulsions on our government to delay vital environmental measures and militarily feasible disarmament.

Again, in order to have decent relations with the rest of the world, we must—and we would under EPI—be able to maintain the high-enough guaranteed level of demand by our own domestic devices. Today we certainly do need to reduce our trade deficit by gaining new export markets, but even if that were a sure way of holding total demand at its high-enough level, which it clearly is not, the other foreign-policy considerations have to be reckoned with, too. It would be not only ignominious but also counterproductive for the most powerful nation on earth to have to ask less well-off developing countries—struggling, and badly in need of markets themselves—to make up to us for a lack of adequate domestic policies here in America.

What else is required? I have never had the illusion that the material, operational change represented by EPI could be implemented without a certain amount of change of heart as well. Economic policies do not operate in a vacuum. Good ones, good procedures, are necessary but they are not sufficient. Could business survive the "chemical" mutation that guaranteed full employment would bring to the employer-worker relationship? Would there still be enough entrepreneurs—could our familiar way of carrying on and producing goods and services hold together once the threat of joblessness was absent? And what about labor's reaction to the effect on wages of the machine-driven eventual necessity for a shorter workweek in order to share the work among more workers?

For my part, I maintain that things would certainly keep going and that there would be plenty of risk and competitive struggle left, and enough slowly evolving public spirit, and a tendency to cooperate.

Index